PENGUIN BOOKS
ROD CAREW'S ART AND SCIENCE OF HITTING

Rod Carew was voted Rookie-of-the-Year in 1967, when he broke in with the Minnesota Twins, and went on to become an All-Star for eighteen consecutive seasons, winning the American League Most Valuable Player Award in 1977, when he hit .388. In 1985, playing for the California Angels, he became the sixteenth player in Major League history to reach the 3,000-hit plateau. Born in Panama in 1945, Rod moved to New York City as a teenager and now lives with his wife, Marilynn, and three daughters in California.

Armen Keteyian is a writer and reporter for *Sports Illustrated* and coauthor with Dave Peck of *Dave Peck's Championship Racquetball System*. Frank Pace is a Los Angeles–based film producer and freelance writer.

Rod Carew's
ART AND SCIENCE
OF HITTING

—————— ◆ ——————

WITH FRANK PACE
AND ARMEN KETEYIAN

PENGUIN BOOKS

PENGUIN BOOKS
Viking Penguin Inc., 40 West 23rd Street,
New York, New York 10010, U.S.A.
Penguin Books Ltd, Harmondsworth,
Middlesex, England
Penguin Books Australia Ltd, Ringwood,
Victoria, Australia
Penguin Books Canada Limited, 2801 John Street,
Markham, Ontario, Canada L3R 1B4
Penguin Books (N.Z.) Ltd, 182–190 Wairau Road,
Auckland 10, New Zealand

First published by Viking Penguin Inc. in simultaneous
hardcover and paperback editions 1986
Published simultaneously in Canada

All photographs by V. J. Lovero except where otherwise indicated.

LIBRARY OF CONGRESS CATALOGING IN PUBLICATION DATA
Carew, Rod, 1945–
Rod Carew's art and science of hitting.
1. Batting (Baseball)   I. Pace, Frank.   II. Keteyian,
Armen.   III. Title.   IV. Title: Art and science of
hitting.
GV869.C36   1986 b   796.357'26   86-4907
ISBN 0 14 00.8516 5

Printed in the United States of America by
R.R. Donnelley & Sons Company, Harrisonburg, Virginia
Set in Century Expanded
Book design by Victoria Hartman
Illustrations by Mary A. Wirth

To Our Wives and Daughters

ACKNOWLEDGMENTS

Over the years, many people have played an important role in my career. It is impossible to acknowledge all of you, but you know who you are, and I thank you.

I'd especially like to acknowledge the following:

Tony Oliva, for all his help in my development as a hitter and as a person;
Dave Garcia, for his professionalism and friendship;
Vern Morgan, for the time he spent with a young player on the way up;
Billy Martin, who taught me the importance of hitting within myself;
Gene Mauch, for being a constant reminder of what I can do, and what I should do;
My teammates;
The 32,000,000 baseball fans who have voted me an All-Star, year in and year out.

A great deal of time and effort has gone into the preparation of this book. Thanks are due to Jerome Simon, Chuck Verrill, John Ware, V. J. Lovero, Steven DeVore of SyberVision, Russell Athletic, Pony Sports and Leisure, Franklin Sports Industries, *Sports Illustrated* magazine, Reggie Jackson of the California Angels, Don Mattingly of the New York Yankees, Don Baylor of the New York Yankees, Wade Boggs of the Boston Red Sox, Tony Gwynn of the San Diego Padres, Steve Garvey of the San Diego Padres, Ron Guidry of the New York Yankees, Dave Smith of the Houston Astros, Tim Mead of the California Angels, Cheryl Pronchick, Andy Strassberg of the San Diego Padres, Gary Adams of UCLA, and Carl Ruhl.

CONTENTS

Rod Carew's
ART AND SCIENCE
OF HITTING

One

◆

INTRODUCTION AND PHILOSOPHY

I love to hit. I always have. Although it's been fun, becoming a good hitter hasn't been easy. I always get a good laugh every time I hear someone say, "Rod Carew is a born hitter; no one can hit like he does." Well, you may not win seven batting titles, but you can become a good hitter, a great hitter, if you want to work at it. I was a sickly child, not born to be a great athlete or to overpower any pitcher, but I worked and worked to draw as much out of my natural ability as I possibly could. I studied the game and paid my dues on countless dusty sandlot fields in Panama and later in the United States; I never stopped thinking, dreaming, about becoming a great hitter. And I challenged myself. No matter how well I hit, how high my average rose, there was—and still is—a little voice inside me saying, "You can do better, Carew . . . you can do better."

Constantly striving to improve is important, but it is important at the start to understand *how* to improve, to grasp the essentials of good hitting. First and foremost, good hitting is doing whatever it takes to help your team win ballgames. That is why you go to the plate—to help your team win. Hitting is personal in the sense that only you can do it for yourself, but it is primarily a function of a team game. The more hits you can get, the more times you'll be on base to score runs, and the more runs you'll drive in. That's obvious. But that's only one aspect of being a good hitter. A good hitter is also an unselfish hitter, one willing to move a runner over, to give himself up, to do the little things that don't always show up in the box score but still have a major impact on the outcome of the game.

It's no coincidence that some of the greatest hitters who ever played the game were unselfish players. Frank Robinson, Steve Garvey, Hank Aaron, and Pete Rose know what it takes to win ballgames; they never gave a moment's thought to making an out if it would advance a runner into scoring position, or to laying down a bunt when the situation called for it. Great hitters know a team's winning percentage is more important than any one player's batting average. So should you. Yet selflessness and desire are only two parts of the equation. Without equal portions of discipline and confidence, you're not going to be a threat at the plate. The late Charlie Lau, hitting instructor for the Royals, Yankees, and White Sox, once wrote, "Rod Carew simply makes solid contact with the ball more often than other hitters." But consistent contact doesn't just happen. It comes from knowing the fundamentals of good hitting and applying them in a disciplined, confident manner. I know what works best for Rod Carew. I know what pitches I like to hit, what pitches I can—and cannot—hit, and where I want to hit every pitch I see. Consequently, I try never to stray from this philosophy, to mess with success. Yet the little laws that established—and now direct—that discipline didn't materialize overnight. It took me years and years of experimentation and self-analysis to decide what was right for me. As someone striving to become—or remain—a .300 hitter, realize you have to make a commitment. Hitting .300 is almost like a cause, a campaign. You can never really rest. You must always strive to learn more about your opponents, to outthink them, to outwork them. In the long run it can only add to your success, but before making this commitment, you must decide what hitting philosophy you will follow.

Over the years, hundreds of different styles, methods, and

theories of how to hit a baseball have developed, but, unfortunately, some instructors remain limited in their knowledge. One may preach strictly "top hand, top hand"—a reference to rolling the top hand over as the barrel of the bat makes contact with the ball—and nothing else. One may preach weight back; another, weight forward; still another, hitting the ball back up the middle. The problem with these theories is that the people who have put them forth speak in absolutes, as if their way is the only way to hit.

This book will occasionally speak in absolutes, but it will not, under any circumstance, stress *one* absolute way, a single concept, of hitting a baseball. Hitting is a multidimensional process. You can learn a little bit from a lot of people. What this book will do is stress the importance of fundamentals and experimentation, and the fact that every hitter is unique. I won't say "Hit like me or else." I don't believe there is any one path to hitting excellence, and it's finally time for me to say so. You only have to look at the disparate styles of a Rickey Henderson, who hits from a pronounced crouch, and a Pedro Guerrero, who stands upright at the plate, to understand that.

I'd have to say there are three players today in the American League who share my approach to hitting, even though our mechanics are slightly different. They are George Brett of the Royals, Don Mattingly of the Yankees, and Texas Ranger first baseman Pete O'Brien. Each of these players is a pure flat-hand hitter. Each starts his approach with his weight already back and lands softly on his front foot; each knows his capabilities as a hitter and uses the whole field. The three of them differ slightly from me in one respect: the setup. Mattingly, for example, has a much more pronounced inward turn of his upper body and, especially, of his front toe. He also stands much more upright than I do in the box. Brett also sets up with his right toe turned inward, but not as much so as Mattingly. George differs in his exaggerated backward lean, which simply means he feels most comfortable in that position and, given his .300-plus career, sees no reason to change. O'Brien, meanwhile, is

George Brett, a two-time batting champion and an MVP, is very similar to me in his approach to the mechanics of hitting. Note how George has his weight back while awaiting the ball. When he strides, he lands softly on his front toe. And George is a "hands" hitter. The primary difference between George and me is that George has a more pronounced closed front toe and a slightly uppercut swing.

In his first four seasons in the big leagues, Don Mattingly has won a batting title and an MVP Award. He is a very flexible hitter at the plate who uses the whole field well. Aside from his power (30-plus home runs and 145 RBIs in 1985), Don is a contact hitter (.324 in '85, .341 in '84) who doesn't strike out much (41 times in 1985). They'd better make room for another monument in center field at Yankee Stadium.

a great young hitter, overshadowed by others because he plays in Texas. He's hit twenty home runs a year with a pretty consistent .280 average the last two seasons, and he seems to be a composite of all three styles (Don's, George's, and mine). O'Brien's lower-body setup is much like Brett's; his upper body is more upright than mine, but not quite as straight as Mattingly's.

On the other hand, I don't think there is anyone more radically different from me in hitting style than are Reggie Jackson and Dave Kingman. They swing at many more pitches than a contact hitter would; they uppercut virtually every pitch. That's why they also strike out a lot. Still, Reggie's one of the greatest home-run hitters of all time, and Kingman also has over 400 home runs to his credit, so don't think I'm being critical of them. But players like Hank Aaron, Babe Ruth, Ted Williams, and now Eddie Murray, Brett, and Mattingly, have proved you can be both a power hitter and a contact hitter.

Williams was certainly a great hitter, one of the greatest of all time, and a fine hitting coach, but I don't agree with everything Ted says about hitting. Ted stressed knowledge of the strike zone, linking batting average to the location of the pitches you swing at. I don't believe in this approach. I believe it's more important to know what pitches you can hit, and where to hit those pitches. To me, knowledge of your *own* hitting zone is more important than knowledge of *the* strike zone. I'm not going to swing at every pitch that arrives between the armpits and the knees just because it's a strike. I'd much rather take a called strike than swing at a pitch I'm not prepared to handle.

So, ultimately, my message is this: I can't hit like Ted Williams any more than you can hit like me. But we can share basic fundamentals and philosophies of hitting in our quest to get the most out of our talents. You'll learn my philosophies, my fundamentals, in this book. But, of equal importance, you'll learn what goes on inside my head, what I think about before a game, in the on-deck circle, in the batter's box, and after every pitch. I feel that in many ways my philosophies are unique, but they are also well grounded. In my twenty years in the major leagues, I've watched thousands of great and not-so-great hitters. I've seen what works and what doesn't, and I've sought to understand the fundamentals of success and failure. I've spent thousands of hours experimenting, watching videotape, refining my own hitting techniques. In the end, I've developed a few basic beliefs, and ten important keys to good hitting. Here they are:

1. *Do not fear the baseball.* The greatest asset any hitter can have is to be fearless at the plate. You can't be afraid of being hit by the ball and be a good hitter.
2. *Stay within yourself.* Know who you are as a hitter, your strengths and weaknesses, and play within your abilities.
3. *Use your hands.* Become an "aggressive hands" hitter. This allows you to wait longer on the pitch and react to changes in pitch direction, both horizontally and vertically in the strike zone.
4. *Be confident at the plate.* Know what you want to do when you get up to home plate. Combine purpose and discipline. Control the confrontation; that is, do what *you* want to do, not what the pitcher wants you to do.
5. *Stay flexible.* You can't be static in the batter's box. You must be able to keep your stance and outlook flexible enough to react to different pitches and situations.
6. *Practice makes perfect.* Work hard to hone your skills, to fine-tune fundamentals. Be willing to pay the price of success, to put in the time necessary to compete against those athletes who pride themselves on a strong work ethic.
7. *Hit the ball where it's pitched.* Learn to utilize the entire field, foul line to foul line. Learn to hit the ball pitched down the middle *through* the middle, to pull the inside pitch, to slap the outside pitch the other way.
8. *Be aggressive.* Swing to make solid contact, to hit through the baseball, remembering not to become so aggressive you begin swinging at bad pitches and start pulling off the ball.

9. *Develop a one-component swing.* Strive to swing in one fluid motion, with all of your body parts functioning together. Avoid the step-turn-swing approach to hitting.
10. *Stay in shape.* Work year round to put—and keep—your body in shape, to draw the most out of your physical abilities.

Fear

A lot of ballplayers are afraid to talk about fear, but it plays a pivotal role in the game, particularly the physical worry of being hit—and perhaps seriously injured—by a pitch. I've never been afraid of getting hit, and that's one edge I have over some other players. Every ballplayer has a general concern about his physical safety—you have to. The sheer speed of some pitchers demands it. But the ones who carry the fear too far, who worry beyond reason, are the ones who get hurt the most. The reason? Simple. They freeze. They don't react. In anticipating a certain pitch, they leave themselves open—thinking curveball and getting a fastball—and when that happens they can't react as quickly, and they take a shot on the shoulder or leg . . . or worse.

To overcome this fear, have a friend throw some rubber balls at you from close range—ten or fifteen feet or so. Remember to react by swinging your back out *toward* the pitcher, thus protecting your face and head. After getting plunked a couple of times with a rubber ball, you'll realize it's going to sting for a second or two, but what the heck, it's part of the game. That's the way my former teammate Don Baylor looks at it. He's been hit by more pitches than any other player in American League history. He just says the heck with it, jogs down to first base, and forgets about it. You must learn to do the same.

Hitting Within Yourself

What kind of hitter are you now? What kind of hitter do you want to be? Does your swing need a complete overhaul or just a little fine-tuning? These are very important questions, one of the reasons "Stay within yourself" is Number 2 in the keys to good hitting. Yet at the same time, these simple questions beg other questions: Are you built for the long ball, and, if so, do you connect or strike out a lot? Did you hit a lot of home runs in Little League or high school but can't seem to connect now? Are you fast but can't seem to hit the ball on the ground to take advantage of your speed? Are you always popping the ball up or pulling the ball into easy outs at short or second?

Before reading any further, sit down and ask yourself these questions. Think of who you are as a hitter and what type of hitter you'd like to be. Are they compatible? Can they ever be? Do you have the body of a Babe Ruth but play the game of a Rickey Henderson? If you can't figure out your problems, consult your parents or your coach. Are you trying to be the type of hitter you just aren't built to be? Analyze yourself; then go about deciding how you would like to change.

Some words of caution: You may not have to alter much at all; maybe what you need is to shift your weight around a bit or get a little more or less aggressive at the plate. But if you do have to change, ask yourself whether you are capable, *mentally*, of making these adjustments. Ego is a tough competitor; if you're too stubborn to admit you can't be the next King Kong of baseball, if you feel you *have* to pull every pitch, well, you may be wasting your time with this book. If you can't adjust when adjustment is necessary, that's fine. Just be prepared to start buying your tickets to baseball games.

Let me give you an example of being too stubborn for your own good. You're a fine, young hitter with one problem: You can't hit the low fastball. Sure enough, soon enough, you strike out on just that pitch, then walk back to the bench muttering to yourself. The next time up, you adjust, which is good, but you make the wrong adjustment. Instead of working on hitting low fastballs in practice you crouch down, attempting to cover the pitch. It doesn't work. A good catcher immediately calls for a high fastball. You swing and miss. So you straighten up.

Then you get a low fastball. Now you're dumbfounded. You don't know what to think or how to stand. Instead of working on your weaknesses—taking batting practice with pitches thrown deliberately down low—you keep shifting around in the box and stay completely confused.

The answer to this problem can be summarized in two words: clear goals. George Brett of Kansas City has clear goals. He knows what he can and cannot do at the plate. Wade Boggs of Boston is the same way. So are the Yankees' Don Mattingly and San Diego's Tony Gwynn. They all accent the positive; they don't pretend to be the hitters they aren't. And it's no mistake they've all won batting titles. On the other side of the coin there are many players consistently mired in the low .200s because they continually kid themselves; they try to be something they're not.

The rise of Gary Pettis really illustrates this point. In 1984 Gary didn't play within himself. He was a free swinger, eager to hit every pitch out of the park. But he was 6 feet, 165 pounds, and it didn't work. For all his big swings, Gary hit 2 home runs, batted .227, and struck out more than 25 percent of the time. Fortunately, after that experience, Gary wised up. He realized he is built for speed, not power, and in 1985 he concentrated on using that speed. He stayed within himself. He hit the ball where it was pitched, and he made contact. In 1985 his average rose to .260; he stole more than 50 bases and established himself as a bona fide major-league hitter. If Gary continues to play under control, I believe he's going to be a great player for many years.

Of course, Pettis should have played to his strengths, to his speed, right away. But it takes time to discover who you are as a hitter and to develop a willingness to change. I'm not saying Gary shouldn't try occasionally to go deep, but one has to weigh his role on the ballclub carefully. Steve Balboni of the Kansas City Royals, for example, knows he's paid to hit the ball out of the park; not, in general, to hit .290. That's for players like his teammate Willie Wilson. So unless you're a young

Dave Winfield, don't try to be someone you're not. Winfield is, of course, another matter; he could help his team, the New York Yankees, by hitting 30 or 40 home runs a year, but he could do even more—as he did in 1984, hitting .340, with 19 homers and 100 RBIs—by staying within himself, not trying for home runs. In Winfield (26 homers, 114 RBIs, .275, in 1985) and in others with such a powerful stroke, like Eddie Murray of Baltimore (31, 124, .297), home runs are simply the frequent result of making such strong, consistent contact with the pitch.

Confidence

It's true that confidence is a by-product of success, but if you're in the proper frame of mind when you walk up to the plate, no matter how well or poorly you've been playing, it's going to have a positive effect on your performance. Throughout my life, from childhood through my career in the major leagues, I've always believed I was going to get a hit. *Every* time up. It has never made any difference to me who is pitching. I want that pitcher to *feel* the confidence I have at the plate; I want every pitcher to know that I'm the best there is and that when I step into the batter's box, he's got his hands full.

I'm also very greedy when it comes to getting hits. I've seen too many players get two hits in their first two at-bats and mentally take the rest of the game off. "My day is made," they say. Not me. When I get two hits, I want three, then four, then five. Conversely, when I make an out, I make an out. I tip my hat to the pitcher, make a mental note of why I failed, and forget about it. But be assured that pitcher knows I'm going to be an even tougher out the next time up.

Baseball is a mental game. There's no way around it. Most ballplayers who fail in the major leagues (and even at lower levels) do so because of weak minds, not weak bodies. Every time you step up to the plate the scene is set: pitcher versus hitter. Somebody is going to win. What you have to learn to guard against is getting too high or too low on any given day, avoiding the peaks and valleys and trying to stay on an even keel. If you're 5 for 5 today and 0 for 5 tomorrow, you have to remember to take each ensuing at-bat individually and not get too complacent or cocky about yourself.

The fear of failure is both the cause and the effect of prolonged slumps. If you don't believe you can hit, you won't hit. It's that simple. Also, if you go into a slump—as all of us do at one time or another—if you lose your confidence, pulling out of the slump will be twice as tough. Both of these psychological problems are much more common in the major leagues than one might believe, because baseball players, like most athletes, for all their bragging and macho image, have very gentle psyches. They bruise easily. Some choose to hide the fear, to mask the emotions with pills, drugs, or alcohol. Psychological fears of this kind are best treated with personal and professional counseling. Another treatable form of fear might be called the "overmatched syndrome." It surfaces most often when playing against the hardest throwers in the game. I've heard my teammates say things like "No use hitting against him tonight," or "We might as well just give him the game." You can't allow yourself to have that attitude, because if it's so-and-so one night, it will be somebody else the next and someone else after that. Pretty soon you've got a built-in bag of excuses for incorrect hitting. Take your cuts, no matter who's throwing or what he's throwing.

Another problem you'll find is that when you do begin to hit well, even in Little League, you become a marked man or woman. Coaches will pitch around you. They'll try to intimidate you, do anything—legal or illegal—to get you off your game. Plus, as you get older and the scouting and managing improve, your swing will be filmed, studied, and broken down like a piece of machinery, with everyone looking for the weak links. It's only a matter of time before someone will realize you don't like, say, a sharp-breaking inside curve, or you will chase a fastball up and out of the strike zone. You just have to realize there are days when you're going to make outs; after all, if you hit

.300, you are still failing seven out of ten times. But you can't stop fixing those weak links, and soon enough they aren't so weak anymore. The only way to do that is with practice. Honest-to-goodness, grimy, T-shirt-soaked-in-sweat practice.

Practice Makes Perfect

For some guys batting practice before a game or on an off day is just an excuse to goof off, to play home-run derby. Personally, I try to hit the ball into the seats only when we're down by a run late in the game and we need runs in a hurry. On the whole, I dislike the long-ball attitude because of what I've seen it do to ballplayers. They get into a game situation where they must move a runner over, hit to the right side, or uppercut a pitch to get a sacrifice fly, and they can't do it. They don't know how to do it. They haven't practiced it.

No matter how I'm hitting, I always take extra batting practice. It doesn't have to be a long drawn-out affair, maybe seven to ten minutes extra on game days and fifteen minutes at other times. But it helps, especially if you use the time wisely. Some days I'll work on a particular pitch I got a hit off the day before but, for some reason, felt funny executing. Maybe I was fooled and fought the ball off; maybe I was a little behind the pitch. Whatever, I'll ask my coaches to keep the ball in that spot during my workout so I can hit that pitch hard and correctly.

Ted Williams, the last of the .400 hitters, had similar theories about extra hitting. He couldn't get enough. Pete Rose is from the same school, and now, I understand, so is Tony Gwynn. That's probably the biggest reason Tony hit .351 in 1984, best in the National League. It was no accident that when his manager, Dick Williams, was asked who would show up to hit at an optional practice during the 1984 World Series, he said, "If only one player showed up, it would be Tony Gwynn."

One final, often overlooked note on batting practice: I've always believed this is a time primarily for working on things you don't do well, leaving a little time to smooth over your strong points. Most players coming out of college today don't work on their weaknesses, a product of their success at lower levels where they were good enough to get by, and even dominate, without worrying about those weaknesses. But in the major leagues, and even in the minors, it's different. Weaknesses are quickly found and continually exploited until the player either adjusts or is replaced.

Purpose and Concentration

No matter what the count, the situation, the surroundings, I've always tried to concentrate, to have a purpose with *every* pitch I've hit. I know sometimes it's impossible; your mind wanders. But it is important that you try to put yourself in an "altered state" whenever you step into the batter's box: a state where school, home, cars, friends, wives, or what you're having for dinner never enters; a state where your mind is focused on just a single object, the *baseball*. Just one white dot with 108 little stitches. You'll find that when your concentration is good, your confidence as a hitter naturally improves. It's also important to forget the past—whether you struck out the time before or if this pitcher reminds you of Nolan Ryan or you have three hits in three at-bats. I can't remember ever being satisfied or complacent about anything I've done in the batter's box. Everything is done for a purpose, and that purpose is making the sweetest, most solid contact you possibly can.

I'm not a big fan of taking pitches. Why wait for the perfect pitch when, first, you may never see it and, second, you lose your aggressiveness waiting for it? If the pitch is *around* home plate and I'm confident I can *handle* it—that is, do something positive with the pitch—I'm swinging. I'm concerned by coaches, especially at lower levels of the game, who tell kids to "wait for a good pitch" before they swing. To me, it's better to learn how to swing the bat and make contact than to wait all day for a pitch down the middle. A pitch may be out of the strike zone, but if you feel you can make solid contact, let 'er rip; especially if you're ahead in the count—2 and 0, 3 and 1—and geared for a certain pitch. Naturally, if you're behind in the count—say, 1 and 2—you have to be less selective.

Over the years I've enjoyed watching certain hitters. One of my favorites was Frank Robinson because he was such a complete hitter. He gave himself up for the team time and time again. He could hit with power and drive the ball deep into the opposite field. Pete Rose and George Brett are fine examples of hitters who play to—and beyond—their abilities. Rose made himself into a hitter, pure and simple, and George—well, George is special because of his concentration, his willingness to use the entire field, and his intense drive, his real hatred of making outs.

Two

◆

SETTING UP THE SWING

Choosing the Right Bat

I have the greatest respect for my bats. I use a 34½-inch-long, 32-ounce bat that is tooled from ash. The top is as wide as the rules allow, giving me a large contact surface. The handle is very narrow, about the width of a 25-cent piece, the combination of fat and thin providing me the proper mix of power and quickness that I desire. But I'm not going to tell you what bat is right for you; there's no golden rule stating if you're this tall and weigh this much, X bat is right for you. It has as much to do with a person's strength, the type of hitter he is (not the type he wants to be), and, in some cases, what bat is available. I do, however, suggest experimenting with various lengths and handle sizes until you find the combination that you like and that works best for you.

But don't expect immediate results. It took me until 1970, my fourth year in the major leagues, to find my bat. Until then I was using heavy, 36-ounce jobs. One day in Lakeland, Florida, I was watching Al Kaline, the Tigers Hall of Fame outfielder and a 3,000-hit man, take batting practice. When Al finished, I asked to see his bat. (It looked as though it bent when he whipped through his swing in the cage.) His bat was very thin and light—just 32 ounces—and very comfortable in my hands. I asked Kaline why he used this model. His answer was simple: It felt good. The same for Harmon Killebrew. He used a 32- or 33-ounce bat, and he could hit a baseball 500 feet. Hank Aaron and Reggie, too. Neither felt he had to tote a tree trunk up to home plate, and they've hit 1,300 home runs between them, with Reggie still counting. So don't get caught up in those mind games that people play, the ones with rules like "The bigger the bat the better the bang." It's a myth.

Bear in mind that the comfortable feel of a bat is the key. For example, I do change bats on occasion, replacing my regular bat late in the season with a shorter, lighter model. The reason is my arms are tired and I don't want to lose any quickness, so I'll sacrifice some weight.

Once you've selected a bat, treat it with respect. I clean all my bats religiously of excess dirt and pine tar so they don't pick up extra weight. Plus, I like the look of a clean bat and a clean, fresh uniform. It says a lot about your sense of pride. And I don't like teammates or strangers picking up or swinging my bats. My feeling is they're my property and I don't want "unauthorized personnel" handling them. On a trip to New York, shortly after I got my 3,000th hit, six of my bats "disappeared" from the locker room at Yankee Stadium. I can't tell you how upsetting that was. Now I'm starting to understand why Pete Rose carries his own bats.

Finally, when it comes to selecting "good wood," I'll let you in on a couple of trade secrets. Look for bats on which the streaks of grain are farthest apart; it's the sign of solid stock. Also, check for a bat with knots on the surface; they're the hardest part of any wood. You can also harden a bat by "boning" it, rubbing the bat along the grain with a hard butcher's bone or another baseball bat. This compresses the wood, making it doubly solid on the surface. Another trick of mine, one unfortunately not available to too many players below the major-league level, is to keep your bats next to a sauna. The dry heat from the sauna bakes out the bad or weak spots in the wood and reduces splintering. In the off-season, I keep my bats in a

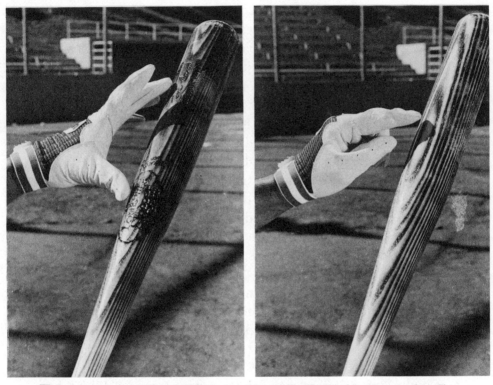

This is a little trick Ted Williams taught me. Earlier in the season, when I'm stronger, I like to use a slightly longer, heavier bat. As the season goes on, I use a lighter, shorter model. But I still want the light bat to seem heavier and longer, and vice versa. To make my shorter bat seem longer, I turn the label side away from me. This way, you see nothing but bat. There is more continuity. When I want my bat to seem shorter and lighter, I face the label toward me. This breaks the continuity of the bat and creates the illusion of a shorter bat. Yes, I know we are talking illusion, but take every advantage you can as a hitter.

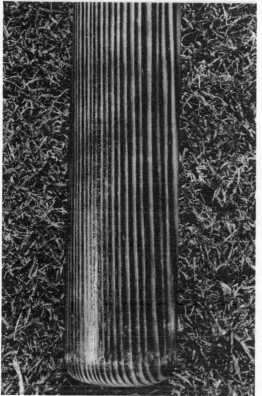

When you select your bats, remember that the wider apart the streaks of grain the better. The grain on this bat is pretty good, but wider would be better.

box filled with sawdust and place them in a warm place in my house. The sawdust acts as a buffer between my bats and the environment, absorbing any moisture before it can seep into the wood.

One final thought: Aluminum bats have taken over on every level of baseball outside the professional ranks, for one reason: It's much more economical to buy bats that last all season than bats that break. But aluminum bats also give you a false sense of accomplishment at the plate. Too many players pick up bad habits because they get base hits off those inside pitches that would have been sure outs with a wooden bat. It's something scouts take into consideration these days when charting a prospect. And I think it's to your advantage, if you have the desire and potential to be a major-league player, to use a wooden bat, if not in a game, at least in batting practice. A wooden bat will show your true talents.

Batting Gloves

Batting gloves are relatively new to the game, and I think they've been an improvement. Certainly, using a glove during batting practice cuts down on the sting after a long session and reduces blisters and calluses on the hands. I'm also in favor of wearing them in the field, as they add a little extra padding. The only caution here is not to get too emotionally tied to your equipment, especially batting gloves. If you happen to lose them or leave them at home, you can't let it affect your play.

The Grip

Ty Cobb choked up on the bat and used a split grip, with a 1-inch gap between the bottom and top hands. His average over 24 major league seasons? Only .363. Mickey Mantle, meanwhile, hit 536 home runs for the New York Yankees in 18 big-league seasons. His grip? The bottom hand so far down the handle of the bat that his pinky finger curled around the bottom of the knob.

The moral to this is that there are no absolutes in gripping a baseball bat. In general, common sense and comfort are the keys to the proper grip. You want to keep things simple, to get the job done without making too big a mess, and there are all sorts of ways to go about it. Most major-leaguers today lean to nothing more than "what's comfortable." That often means holding the bat in an area of the hands where the palm ends and the fingers begin, the alignment no more complex than lining up your knuckles. By that I mean that the knuckles on the first joint of each hand should be in a line. There is nothing wrong with this grip except that it's the only grip many coaches teach.

If aligning the knuckles is not comfortable, experiment and find a grip that is, and that's not hard to do. Just pick up your bat and let your fingers do the talking. Be as natural as possible, not putting the bat too far forward in your fingers or too

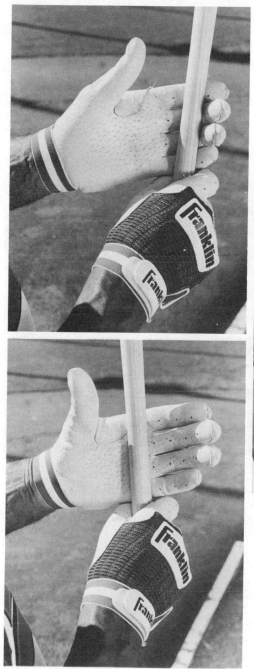

Find a grip that is comfortable for you. I prefer the bat loosely held toward my fingers. Other players like the bat in either the front or back part of their palms. There is no right and wrong way. Experiment with the bat and find out what feels right for you.

Notice how the knuckles in my grip do not line up. Compare this to the photo where my knuckles are lined up. See the difference. Most coaches teach lining up the knuckles. That doesn't make them right, or me right. What's right is what works for you.

far back in your palms. Imagine playing a trumpet or saxophone. Feel the wood; don't grip the bat too tightly. Tension is your enemy, and in one easy lesson I can show you why.

Make a fist with either hand. Look at the inside of your wrist, at the tendons. See the strain? Feel the tightness? Of course you do. Now pull your fingers into a fist but don't hold so tightly. See the difference when you look at your wrist? That extra tension inhibits your ability to generate bat speed because the wrists and forearms—sources of hand speed and power—are tied into knots.

My preference is to grip the bat very lightly with my bottom hand. My bottom hand (since I hit from the left side, my right hand) exerts very little pressure, acting almost like a rudder to keep my swing on course. Meanwhile, my top hand holds the bat handle loosely, tightening as the pitch leaves my opponent's hand. The top hand should *never* clamp down hard on the bat; rather it should maintain a firm grip. This makes you (A) a more relaxed hitter and (B) a more flexible hitter, capable of maneuvering the bat quickly and efficiently through the strike zone.

It is equally important to take care of your hands (I've made a great living with mine). Treat them carefully, lovingly. I never go around smashing my hands into water coolers; I don't attack lockers or walls. Those are fights you cannot win. On the bat, I hold them loosely, free of tension, believing if you're going to squeeze the bat upon contact anyway, why force the issue? Keeping my hands loose allows me to maneuver the bat better, decreases upper-body tension, and it allows me to attack certain pitches that, if my hands were wrapped tightly around the lumber, I'd never get to in time.

Once you're settled on a grip, it's time to figure out where you want to place your hands on the bat. Personally, I advocate choking up a bit, moving your hands up off the bottom. This not only quickens and shortens the stroke but increases your maneuverability.

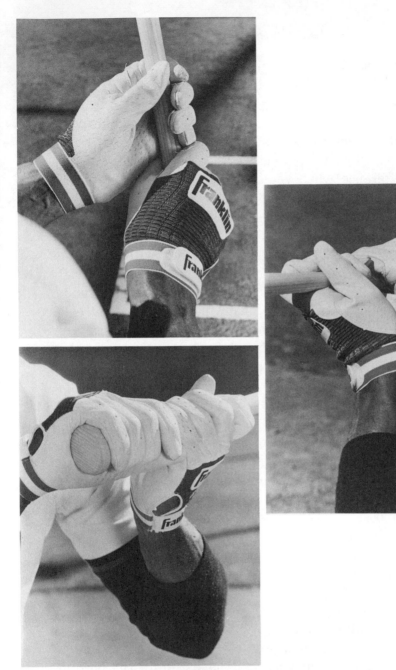

From these three angles, you can see how softly I hold the bat. My bottom
hand is relaxed and exerts very little pressure on the bat. My top hand is
doing little more than cradling the bat. Neither hand will tighten its grip
until just prior to contact. Loose hands are the source of hand speed.

Choking Up on the Bat

One of the remnants of baseball's past that hasn't survived too well in the last thirty years is the style of "choking up"—moving the hands up—on the bat. Though today's players may be better athletes, the old-timers were on to something when they decided to choke up.

Baseball history was written by men like Ty Cobb and Wee Willie "Hit-'em-where-they-ain't" Keeler, choke-up artists who lived by one rule: To get a hit, you first had to hit the ball. In recent years, only Rose and my ex-teammate Tim Foli come to mind as players who consistently move their hands more than an inch or two off the bottom of the bat. Interesting, isn't it, how the name Rose once again meets that of Cobb on the same printed page?

Anyway, a hitter who chokes up on the bat has to accept the fact that he is not a home-run hitter. Pete Rose once said that he wanted to be the first singles hitter to drive a Cadillac. He ended up driving a Rolls-Royce, so you'd have to say that hitting singles has been very good to him. With more than 3,000 singles to his credit, Pete is baseball's all-time leader in that category. [Editor's note: Carew is sixth, with 2,402.]

Choking up on the bat gives you more good wood to work with. It also makes the bat shorter, and though this limits your reach somewhat, it makes you concentrate harder to lay off marginal pitches that you can't drive. It's interesting to see how that extra concentration makes better hitters of players who do shorten up on the bat after they have two strikes. If they hit all the time as they do with two strikes, they'd probably hit 20 points higher.

How much should you choke up? Like most other things in hitting, there is no definitive answer. Play with the bat and find an area that feels comfortable for you. You're obviously not going to choke up to the label, but two or three inches should begin to get you into the comfort zone. And don't worry about what the other kids will say. I'd rather choke up and

Choking up can help a hitter make better contact, and I'm all in favor of that. Not only does it give a hitter better bat control, but for some reason a player seems to concentrate more when he chokes up.

play all the time than swing from the end of the bat and sit on the bench. Just in case you're wondering, I don't choke up myself, but that's only because I like to have the extra bat length, and I feel confident and comfortable knowing what pitches I can hit, and that I will make good, consistent contact without choking up.

Three

THE STANCE

Think of a marvelous meal set on a beautiful, colored tablecloth made of fine linen, with shining silver and sparkling crystal. Then imagine rushing through this meal at breakneck speed, not enjoying either the food or the setting.

You can't believe how many ballplayers fire through their at-bats at the same speed. Instead of taking their time, setting up in the box, enjoying the meal, they rush right through an at-bat as if they were eating in a fast-food restaurant. *Your stance is the foundation of your swing. Take your time.* Don't treat it lightly. You must not feel silly, particularly in the early stages of a stance adjustment, in taking a few extra seconds in the batter's box. You should always run down a little mental list: Are the feet set? Can you cover the plate with your bat? And don't feel foolish if from time to time you have to step out of the box, back away from the plate, and tinker with your stance to make sure you're comfortable. Just do it. The game will wait.

Over the years much has been said and written about my style of hitting, about the different positions I assume in the box, how I move around from at-bat to at-bat, from pitch to pitch. It's certainly true that, on occasion, I adjust my stance from pitcher to pitcher, even pitch to pitch, but I would like to lay to rest one of the biggest misconceptions about my stance:

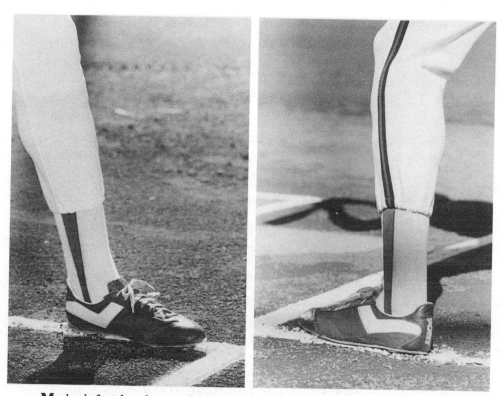

My back foot hasn't moved from this spot in years. I like to set up deep in the batter's box, to get a longer look at the ball, and close to home plate, to get maximum plate coverage. I'm not concerned about being jammed, because that is determined by the position of your front foot, not your back foot.

I do not move around in the batter's box. My back foot hasn't moved in twelve years. Only my front foot moves, shifting open or closed in relation to the situation at hand.

Because of this misconception, some have said I'm the only person who can hit "on the move." Nonsense. If a young hitter wanted to work at it and find the comfort I've found, using what I call the flexible stance, fine. Stronger players in general don't make big adjustments in their stances—Baylor has always hit straight up with a slightly closed stance, and Reggie is open a bit, swinging from his heels—but to be a consistent hitter, I believe you need to be able to adjust, to adapt your game to the pitcher. The changes are not major; normally I make some minor mechanical adjustments, not to the *kind* of pitch but to the location of it. This gives me a much better chance of seeing the baseball. But you just can't use any stance for a day, a week, or two weeks and expect big results. I've worked with guys who have tried one stance, found it comfortable, then had a bad day or two. The first change they make is right back to their old way of hitting, and in their haste and insecurity, they never really give themselves a chance to become comfortable—and confident—with this crucial part of the hitting process.

The Carew Flex-Stance

As with any good, solid stance, the flex-stance begins with your feet. They should generally be about shoulder width apart, facilitating an easy weight transfer from the back foot to the front as the ball approaches what I call the "contact zone." For me, the contact zone means the area just off the front foot, about a foot in front of the plate. Just how far the contact zone extends out in front of home plate depends on the location of the pitch. But the general rule of thumb is this: The location of the pitch from outside to inside is in direct proportion to how far out front you want to make contact. In other words, if the pitch is outside, wait a split second longer before swinging. If it's down

The contact zone is that area just off your front foot, and in front of home plate, where the bat meets the ball. To keep the ball in play, you must contact the ball *in front of home plate*. The farther in front of home plate your bat is upon contact, the more you will pull the ball. The closer you are to the front of home plate upon contact, the more you will hit to the opposite field.

the middle, attack a bit earlier, and even earlier for an inside pitch.

The reasons are many: First, the deeper a ball gets into the strike zone, the harder it is to hit it fair. Second, as mentioned, the most wicked movement on fastballs and curves often comes in the last two to three feet before it reaches the plate. Finally, your hands and hips come into play in front of the plate. If you're slow, if the ball gets "in" on you, your body tightens, you lose arm extension, and you can't get the fat part of the bat on the ball. In short, your license to drive the ball has been taken away. So, to keep the ball in play, to move it around the diamond, to hit the best part of a pitch, contact the ball *out in front of the plate.*

Also, much has been written about the need for having a "balanced" stance, as opposed to leaning too far forward on your front foot or too far backward on your rear foot. The need to be balanced is one of the biggest misconceptions of good hitting. I'm not a "balanced" hitter, never have been, at least not during my setup in the box. I like to hit out of a slightly coiled stance, with my weight shifted back, so that when I pick up the pitch, I can move forward into a comfortable, controlled, balanced swing position. In a so-called balanced stance, you begin with your weight already evenly distributed, but when the baseball is released, you have to lean back a bit in order to push forward, to generate the power necessary to open the hips and push off the legs. Why not eliminate excess movement and try to start in a setup position with your weight already back?

Where to Stand

Okay, we've decided how we're going to distribute our weight. Now, where do you place the back foot? For this, there are as many opinions as there are fans in the stands. Some people prefer to stand deep in the box, others want to remain even with the plate, and still others prefer to have their front foot beyond the front edge of home plate. Once that decision has been made, you must decide how close to the plate you want to be. Are you better off standing on top of the plate? A few inches or a few feet away?

Whatever the final decision, remember: In every one of these situations you're giving up something to get something. Stand close to the plate and you'll certainly get coverage on the outside corner, but, inevitably, you'll find yourself in a position to be worked to death inside. And what about having that front foot so far forward as to be beyond the plate? Great for hitting the curve before it breaks, but trouble when a guy has a 90-mph fastball that he can cut any way he wants. My advice is this: Move your back leg along the back line, near the *inside* chalk mark of the box. This places you deep in the box and fairly close to home plate, giving you time to wait on the pitch. With a flexible *front* leg, you have the ability to adjust, to open or close the stance, depending on the pitcher, and even, at times, the pitch.

I know, I know. A lot of you out there don't like that advice. You think hitting that far back in the box or that close to the plate limits your ability to hit the curveball, but in my experience pitchers with good curves can break it off either in front or in back of the box. (They just shorten or lengthen their delivery.) Thus the front-of-the-box argument is a weak one. For me, staying back buys me time, time to see the pitch, the type and the direction. By increasing my reaction time, it gives me a chance to adjust to surprises.

Now, with this back leg planted, we can get into the main distinctions of the flex-stance. The key to this stance is the front foot. I treat my back foot as a hinge and my front foot as a gate to swing open and closed, depending on who's pitching and what he throws.

My standard stance from the flex position is medium open, my front leg anywhere from 8 to 12 inches from the inside chalk line. This allows me to turn my head so that both eyes face the pitcher, making for good sight lines on most of the pitches thrown. I use this stance 80 percent of the time.

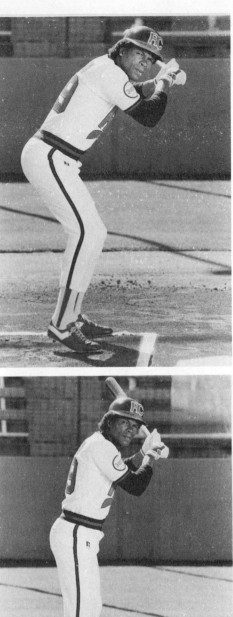

The three basic stances you'll want to experiment with are the opened stance, which I use 80 percent of the time, in which the back foot is far closer to the plate than the front foot. Next is a straight-away stance, with both feet parallel to the near edge of the plate. And then the closed stance, in which the front foot is closer to the plate than the back foot. Experiment, too, with a crouch and a straight-up stance, as I am in the photos. Go with whatever is comfortable . . . and works. But remember that whether your stance is opened or closed, your stride still must be directly toward the pitcher.

The front foot, meanwhile, is not lying flat on the ground like most players'. Rather, my heel is elevated about two inches, a change I made in 1972 because I didn't feel I was getting enough mobility in my hips and legs, and I wanted to be able to "turn" on a pitch more quickly. With my heel up, my pivot off that front toe is much faster, because I don't have to raise my foot to turn. Also, when I stride, I don't come down heavily on that front foot but land softly on the toes, which allows me to increase my leverage and open up more quickly on inside pitches. The front leg is straight but somewhat loose, just firm enough to support the hip rotation but not rigid. If I commit that leg, locking it, my flexibility is lost, and I can't adjust to the ball's inside or outside movement. The only time that the leg should lock is *after* contact is made and the hands are released. The two other key positions of the flex-stance are as follows:

Open. Front foot 12 to 18 inches off the inside chalk. Used in situations where the pitcher regularly throws inside or when facing a sidearm curveball pitcher who throws from your side of the plate.

Closed. Front foot closer to the chalk line, almost parallel to the back foot. Used principally against pitchers who consistently paint the outside corners or have a fastball or slider that runs away from the hitter.

Important: Because your front foot is mobile, and because it is natural to fear the baseball, the tendency is to "pull out," to take your first step away from home plate regardless of whether your stance is open or closed. This is wrong. Don't give in to the temptation. That first step should *always* be right back up the middle, right back at the pitcher. This discourages the disastrous tendency, particularly in the medium and open stances, to pull off a pitch, which in turn takes your head and shoulders out, away from the ball.

When to Be Flexible

You can use all three stances in the same at-bat, but the real key is obviously knowing when to make your move. Baseball is not a computer sport. You don't punch up one key and always get the same answer. It's a subtle science, with a pitcher mixing three, maybe four excellent pitches he can spot wherever he wants, working in concert with a catcher whose job it is to think one step ahead of the hitter, to keep the batter off balance and powerless. As I said before, I'm not a guess hitter; rather, I'm more of a situational hitter, a "tendency" hitter, someone who is prepared with a working knowledge of the pitcher I am facing *before* I step up to the plate. I study my opponents and know, in advance, what they like to throw, *where* they like to throw it, and *when* they like to throw it. In major-league baseball it's obviously easier to make these judgments, to pick up patterns. We know, on a day-to-day basis, who we'll be facing, and our teams all have scouting departments to help prepare us on just what to expect from our opponents. And if they don't know, chances are someone in the dugout has played with or against this new face somewhere along the line in college or the pros. So we can pick up his pattern fairly quickly, if he hasn't changed.

But that's not to say you can't do a little scouting of your own. You have to if this flex-stance is going to work. Certainly you can watch the opposing pitchers warm up in the bullpen before the game. Even from afar, you'll notice whether they throw predominantly fastballs or off-speed pitches. Also, look to see how they pitch to the first few batters. Do they try to set them up, or do they go with the hard stuff? Are they afraid to pitch inside? Do they like to throw a sinker or curveball when they're ahead in the count? When do you see the fastball? Also, talk to your teammates hitting ahead of you in the lineup and check out the movement of pitches thrown to them. By doing this, you'll walk into the batter's box prepared, knowing

I use this stance, from the flex position, about 80 percent of the time. My weight and hands are back, my back foot firmly planted for support, and my front heel raised about 2 inches to allow me to open, close, rise, or go down into the pitch.

what stance to use. You'll be hitting from a position of strength, not weakness.

Usually, however, no matter who's pitching, I like to start out with my medium-open stance, adjusting as I see fit. In some situations, that may be the next pitch, if the first pitch happens to be called a strike and I know, from experience, that when this pitcher is ahead early in the count he tends to throw the curveball inside. So I'll move that front gate, that foot, open a bit, allowing myself a little extra room inside to turn on the pitch. But, again, I'm not guessing curveball, just the tendency of this pitcher to come inside. Even with the slightly more open stance, because I'm always stepping straight toward the mound, I should be able to handle any pitch.

Mind Games

Can you dictate from the setup position what kind of pitch you want thrown? Absolutely. I feel if he's thinking, any hitter can set up a pitcher. Why not? They do it to us all the time. Take Tommy Davis, the former Los Angeles Dodger outfielder and a batting champion, for instance. I saw him set guys up for years. A pitcher would throw Tommy a breaking ball and he would take a bad swing on purpose, knowing full well that in certain game situations he would want the pitcher thinking he could get him out on that same curve. Many a time I saw the guy come back with a curve and Tommy hit the ball hard to win a game.

With this flex-stance it's possible to dictate pitches without sacrificing a swing or a turn at bat. On the occasions when I've wanted a pitch on the inside of the plate, I've leaned over with my hands and head and closed my front foot a couple of inches. When the pitcher and catcher see this, they invariably think "fastball inside." They think I'm afraid of not reaching the outside for the pitch. But as soon as the ball leaves the pitcher's hand and I see it's coming to the inside corner, I'm ready to open up that front leg and turn on the ball. Even if I don't pull it, I can still get good wood on the pitch and hit it up the middle or to the opposite field.

Now, what happens when pitchers wise up to this maneuver and use some reverse psychology on you? What if he sees your adjustment, knows you're really looking for an inside pitch, and keeps the ball outside? Simple. You don't do a thing. Just swing away. That is the beauty of the flexible front foot. If you can learn to pick up the ball soon enough (something I'll discuss in the next chapter), you should be able to stay one step ahead of your enemy, because a pitcher can't change location once he's delivered a pitch. That's when you make your move.

You can also learn to set the pitcher up with your stance at the plate. Maybe I'll crouch a bit lower or stand up a bit straighter in my stance if the pitcher tends to aim for one particular level of the strike zone. I could be standing straight, but when he gets ready to pitch I might bend my knees a little. I do this spontaneously now, because it's something I've experimented with for many years and I feel comfortable with it. But for you my suggestion would be to practice three or four different stances in batting practice, working during practice to adjust those stances as the pitcher is about to deliver.

I know what you're thinking. There are a million different combinations of stances. How do you decide what stance is right in what situation? What I do is limit myself to three or four basic stances that, given the starting pitcher and the relievers the opposing team has, I anticipate using that day. I also work on hitting pitches in certain directions off certain stances. For example: From an upright stance, I'll force myself to hit on top of the ball. Or let's say a sinkerball pitcher is working, a pitcher who keeps the ball down around the knees. I have a preset plan of what I want to do, which is to adjust my stance *down*, not move my front leg in or out. Because of the sinkerball, I'll crouch a little more at the plate to get down to the level so I can see the ball better and handle the pitch. The reason is simple. If the pitcher is throwing sinkers on the outside corner and I'm standing straight up, there's no way I can get good wood on that pitch. That's the problem with hitters who set up very straight, like Don Baylor. They don't have the flexibility in their legs to go down and get a pitch.

Of all the players I've seen, Don Mattingly is the most flexible. He's been able to make adjustments in his hitting approach not only during a ballgame but during an at-bat. Let me share a story with you about Mattingly that happened during the 1985 season. Late in the season, both of our teams were involved, unsuccessfully as it turned out, in a heated pennant race. As so often happens, the Angels went out and purchased some late-season pitching help. In this case, it was John Candelaria, a hard-throwing left-handed pitcher who had been a twenty-game winner for the Pirates in the National League. Whenever you are seeing a pitcher for the first time, the pitcher has the advantage, and the game we were playing in was Candy's debut against the Yankees. To make things doubly difficult, Candelaria has a three-quarter-sidearm delivery, which is very intimidating to left-handed hitters.

During this particular game, in the middle innings, Mattingly came to the plate for a second time against Candy. I noticed he had altered his stance from the previous at-bat. Naturally this interested me. He had closed his right shoulder substantially, and I couldn't wait to talk to him about it. Don walked during that at-bat, so, as he stood on first, he and I talked about his strategy. He told me he had found that during his first at-bat he had a tendency to want to release his upper body too soon against the left-handed sidearm offerings of Candelaria, so as he stepped in to face him a second time, he decided he would close his upper body—by that I mean he would show more of his back to the pitcher. This, he felt, would force him to keep his front shoulder in longer and would delay his "mechanics"—the movements of his swing—making him wait longer on the curveball and slider. I'm not sure Don's adjustment was correct, but he was thinking properly, and as he sees more and more of Candelaria and continues his experimenta-

You have to learn to keep your body on the same plane as the ball. Keeping your legs flexible is the key. Look at how my legs control my approach into a low and outside pitch. As my legs glide down and into the ball on my stride, my whole body calmly comes with them. When I make contact, my center of gravity is lower, but still equally balanced.

tion, I have no doubt he'll hit .330 against Candy, as he does against the rest of the league.

One of the most important points relative to the flex-stance is that you remain, as much as possible, on the same plane as the ball. By this I mean that you can't very easily swing up on a pitch that's down, or conversely, swing down on a pitch that's up in the strike zone. In general, if a pitch is right down the middle, belt high, your swing should be perfectly flat. If the pitch is down at the knees or below, you shouldn't bend at the waist to hit it but rather use your flexible legs to move your entire body in line to hit that pitch. And you can't be down in a crouch and bounce up to go after a high pitch. If you do, nine times out of ten you'll find yourself either swinging and missing, taking a bad swing, or popping the ball up. You have to let your legs adjust to your body or learn to lay off a pitch that's not on your plane.

Obviously, the one time you can't afford to lay off is with two strikes and a borderline pitch that could be strike three. You have to swing. But, in that case, with two strikes you wouldn't want to anticipate too much, crouching so low you couldn't swing and at least foul off a higher pitch that could be borderline. Good hitters spoil good pitches. This can sometimes disrupt a pitcher's concentration because when he knows that you can spoil his best pitch in a crucial situation, he will really have his work cut out for him.

Some of the setup position is personal preference—that is, "what's comfortable"—but understand some basic do's and don't's: Hold your bat too high and you'll find that as time goes on, as the pitching gets faster and more sophisticated, you'll be late getting the bat into the contact zone. Hold your hands too low and you'll have to move them up to get into hitting position. This wastes time, time you don't have, particularly against power pitchers. Hold your hands too close to the body and you'll find yourself "tied up," not being able to get the bat head into the contact zone. You're also inviting yourself to see a steady

To get yourself on the same plane as a ball that is up in the strike zone, you don't want to go down and then up into the ball with your stride. Use your legs, as I use mine in this sequence, to bring you up and keep you there.

diet of inside fastballs that will crack more than their fair share of bats in two. Most ballplayers seem to find common ground with their hands back, about even with their back shoulder, top hand near the tip of their shoulder.

Four

$\blacklozenge$

READING THE SPIN

Tennis players call it being "in the zone." In baseball, it is often described in less cosmic but certainly no less meaningful terms. When we're "seeing the ball," the results are often out of this world: four- and five-hit games, twenty-game hitting streaks, a home-run rampage. For some reason, when you're "seeing the ball," it's bigger; you pick it up sooner; your reactions are quick and direct. Faster reading of spin tips off what kind of pitch is on the way, giving you an extra and valuable advantage over other hitters. And it's not that difficult. It takes concentration, observation, and the ability to master a few common rules.

Many ballplayers get into the habit of playing mind games with the pitcher and catcher. Of course, it's important to know what a guy has thrown, what he can throw; it alerts you to what's coming. And, sure, pitchers do throw in patterns—though, because of better coaching, not as much as they did ten or fifteen years ago. In the old days, you wouldn't see a change-up or breaking ball on 3-2 or 2-2. Now I see screwballs on 3-2, changes on 3-0 or 3-1, forkballs on 2-0. Of course, in Little League, junior high, and high school, the patterns are more predictable, though much depends on the pitcher himself. Does he want to get ahead of the hitter? Can he get his curve over for a strike? In high school, pitchers often don't have any idea of how they want to pitch. So it is best to anticipate their best pitch in a clutch situation. Why? It's a pitch they can control, and they don't want to get hurt with less than their best stuff. But beware: This isn't easy. If you're guessing the wrong pitch, you can't adjust. So, don't guess, at least not at the type of pitch. It's all right to look for location, but I, for one, always look for one pitch: the fastball. I prepare myself mentally and physically for it on every delivery, for one basic reason: It moves at upward of 90 miles an hour, and reacting to it takes the ultimate in hand-eye coordination. Every other pitch is slower, be it a slider, curve, screwball, or change-up. If you're geared to hit a fastball, you can easily delay your mechanics to allow for a slower pitch. If, however, you're "sitting on"—guessing at, waiting for—a 70-plus-mile-an-hour curveball, there is no way you can accelerate your mechanics quickly enough to react to a faster pitch. So, anticipate fastball and allow your reactions, your patience, and your discipline to handle everything else.

Rule No. 1: Know Where to Look

Every pitcher has a release point, the point at which the ball leaves his hand, and it is the exact spot at which a hitter should begin to read the pitch. With few exceptions, the most successful pitchers release all their pitches from the same spot. This is a mixed blessing, in that the hitter knows exactly where to look for every pitch, but, then again, the pitcher is able effectively to camouflage his pitches. You will find pitchers, especially at lower levels, who tip their pitches by releasing different pitches from different points. The fastball is released over the top, by the ear; the curveball is released lower, almost at three quarters; or vice-versa. In this case, it's your job to learn the release point of each pitcher you face. If a pitcher is nice—or rather foolish—enough to tip his pitches, you should be wise enough to take advantage of it, by watching his warmup, talking to other hitters, studying his mechanics.

The pitcher's release point is simply the point where the ball leaves his hand. Good pitchers do not vary their release point from pitch to pitch. It is from the release point that I first begin to read the spin of a pitch.

Release points differ from pitcher to pitcher. This is what the release point might look like from a sidearm/submarine pitcher. Ignore the motion, watch the release point, and this type of pitcher is no more difficult to hit than any other.

It takes only half a dozen pitches or so to figure out where the fastball is released from and how, if at all, the release point may differ from that of his other pitches. Even if you're the leadoff hitter, by your second at-bat you should pretty much have the pitcher pegged. And—just between you and me—keep an eye on your own pitchers. In most cases, they will not be your teammates for life. You'll probably be opponents some-day, whether it's in American Legion, high school, college, or the pros. It doesn't hurt to have some personal information on that pitcher filed away in your head for down the road.

Rule No. 2: Know When to Look

Some players say the best way to pick up the baseball is to watch the entire motion from start to finish. Never take your eyes off the pitcher, they say. Not me. If you stare too long at the mound, you become mesmerized, so I never concentrate on the ball when it's in the pitcher's glove. Instead, while the pitcher is just standing on the rubber, I'm preparing myself at the plate, relaxing my hands, working on my rhythm. I'll remain in that mode, and as the pitcher winds, I draw both my hands and front foot back, setting up my swing. Only *after* the hands break from the glove do I pick up the ball. From there, I go straight to the release point, where I again pick up the ball. Within fifteen to twenty feet after the ball has been released, I have computed the spin and know whether a fastball or an off-speed pitch is on the way. Don't think for a second this is some simple equation. It's not. You have to *concentrate*. Often you find a pitcher who can make the ball dance, moving it up or down or in or out. Thus, it's important to know the characteristics of every pitch—how, for example, a slider moves about 10 miles an hour slower than a fastball, breaking about three feet from home plate. The more you know about a pitch, the quicker you can decide what to do with it, and the longer you can wait.

I first pick up the ball when the pitcher breaks his hands for the last time in his delivery. Once I see the ball in his hand, my eyes go directly to the pitcher's release point.

And—the key to all this—the longer you wait on a pitch, the better hitter you'll be.

Reading the Spin

The prospect of picking out rotation on a baseball from a distance of some 55 feet, traveling at a speed approaching 90 mph, is enough to boggle the mind. And well it should. If that isn't tough enough, few ballplayers, particularly at the lower levels, know *what* to look for, even if they are looking. They don't know how a certain pitch rotates when thrown, say, across the seams, or how a curve or slider spins. Reading the spin is a delicate science. But once you begin to master it, the rewards are worth all the effort. You'll begin seeing the ball earlier and earlier, enabling you to program your mind faster, allowing you to wait longer before making a decision to swing. You'll also stop chasing pitches out of the strike zone. With all these possibilities in mind, let's discuss the specific spin on the most common pitches.

Fastball

The fastball comes in two varieties. One is thrown with the fingers gripping the ball across the seams, the other with the pitcher gripping the ball *with* the seams. Each pitch shares one particular trait: As the ball approaches home plate, the seams of the baseball are spinning from the bottom upward—because, with the fastball, the ball is rolling off a pitcher's fingers, causing the ball to spin backward, toward the pitcher. The upward spin causes the ball to rise because air is flowing under the ball faster than it is flowing over the ball. This is the same principle that allows an airplane to fly. Most pitchers throw their fastballs across the seams, and that's the fastball that will tend to rise most.

Facing a fastball thrown *with* the seams, you may notice how the ball will appear "lighter" in color, because you are seeing only two seams spin rather than all four. Although the spin of this pitch is still upward, it will be somewhat angular; the ball will move into a right-hander if thrown by a righty and away from him if thrown by a lefty. It won't rise as much as a fastball thrown across the seams.

Curveball

When the curveball is properly thrown, the spin is the opposite of that on a fastball, meaning the ball will sink, not rise. Downward spin is generated when the pitcher comes straight over the top on his release and pulls down on the ball, snapping his wrist sharply upon release.

If you look hard enough, you'll also notice the spin on the curve will be looser, more visible to the naked eye than that of the fastball. Why? Simple. You can't throw the pitch as hard. The difference you'll notice from a pitcher with a three-quarter release as opposed to one over the top is that rather than spinning straight downward, the curve will angle slightly. On a clock it would spin from the 2-o'clock position if thrown by a righty or the 10-o'clock position if thrown by a lefty. This causes the ball to move not only down but away from a righty if thrown by a righty.

Slider

The slider is a tough pitch to judge because many pitchers throw it from different locations. The primary difference between the slider and the curve is that the slider has a tighter spin (faster revolutions), and has a more sudden, more horizontal movement. Many players say that the combination of the tight, downward, cross-seam spin causes a small dot to form on the baseball where all four seams meet—so look for that. It's just an optical illusion, and not all batters pick it up, but if you can, you'll find it easier to recognize the pitch. Another thing to remember about the slider is that it's moving quicker than a curveball but not quite as quick as a fastball. When thrown by a right-hander, the pitch will break 6 to 8 inches out and away from a right-handed hitter (or into a lefty). If thrown at belt level, it's a nice pitch to hit; but if it's coming in down and away, the way former twenty-game winner Andy Messersmith threw it, try to leave it alone, because by the time you get to it, chances are it will be out of the strike zone. Of course, if it's a borderline two-strike pitch, try to fight it off or hit it foul. A lot of times you're just not going to be able to hold up and you're going to wind up swinging at a ball. Just accept it and be ready for the next one.

Split-Finger Fastball
The split-finger fastball has achieved a certain cult status lately, thanks in part to the success of Bruce Sutter and, later, students of Roger Craig (now manager of the Giants) such as Jack Morris and Dan Petry. The split-finger pitch is used as a change-of-pace pitch, even though it is actually quite fast, as little as 5 miles an hour slower than a fastball. This pitch looks like a slider, but at the last instant, instead of moving horizontally, it suddenly drops. The best way to battle it is to stay back and not commit your hands until you're sure the pitch is going to stay in the strike zone.

Change-Up
A good change should always be thrown off the fastball motion, with the same arm speed and the same release point, the only difference being velocity. There's also a variation of the change, the "circle change"—so named because it's thrown by encircling the ball between the thumb and forefinger. As the pitcher pulls down on the ball, you get the same spin as the fastball,

Note: All pitches seen from batter's point of view, as if thrown by a right-handed pitcher

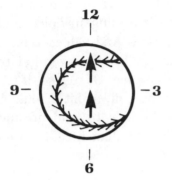

Fastball spin:
when thrown across the seams

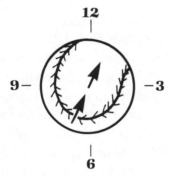

Fastball spin:
when thrown with the seams
(spin direction of
a "cut fastball"
is much the same)

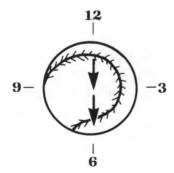

Overhand curve:
Spin is nearly
12 o'clock to 6 o'clock
when properly thrown.

Slider:
tighter rotation and
more revolutions
than the curveball;
sharper sideward break,
toward 4 o'clock

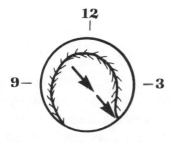

Split-finger fastball:
curveball-type spin with
near-fastball velocity

but little of the speed. (The pitch rarely climbs over 80 mph on the radar gun.)

If you're anxious and trying to pull the change—especially if it's on the outside corner, where it belongs—all you'll hit are easy ground-outs. So wait and try to take it back up the middle or to the opposite field. You"ll probably end up pulling it anyway, but pulling it fair instead of foul.

Can't Read Spin? Look for Location

Some people just don't have the eyesight or the ability to read spin. If you don't, look location. Pick up the ball upon its release and compute whether it's going to be inside, outside, high, low, or down the middle. Once you've come to some kind of decision, prepare yourself mentally—and mechanically—for a pitch in that spot. *But don't overcompensate.* That's the worst thing you can do. Anticipate, yes. But don't lean so much in one direction that you're helpless if the pitcher, say, misses the anticipated spot. It's all right to feel, on a 1-2 count, that the pitch will be coming inside, and to have the bat ready. But don't start leaning back or opening up before the ball reaches you. Be patient and concentrate.

Making Adjustments

As I've said, if you're smart, you can learn to use your body to limit the strengths of opposing pitchers and force them to play your game. The key is automatically knowing, once you see a certain style of pitcher, how to handle him. Certainly you can, if you feel confident enough, match your best against his. But my advice is don't, on any occasion, say, crouch deeply in the box against a heralded curveballer just because someone tells you that's the best way to hit that type of pitcher. You know yourself better than anyone. You make the decisions. But before you do, take these specific situations into consideration.

Hard thrower on the mound, coming over the top. When a pitcher comes over the top, his fastball rises and seems to pick up speed as it approaches the plate. Therefore, pitches up in the strike zone are faster, more difficult to track—and to hit. My adjustment in this situation is to crouch a bit to bring my strike zone down, in turn forcing the pitcher down—and thereby decreasing the rising movement on his fastball, theoretically making it easier for me to see and hit. That's one of the reasons I've enjoyed success against Nolan Ryan over the years; I've

This is my coiled stance. I'll use this against a hard thrower, like Nolan Ryan, who throws a rising fastball. A rising fastball can overpower any hitter when it gets up in the strike zone. This stance forces the pitcher to bring the ball lower in the strike zone, away from his power up. I'll also use this coiled stance when I want to try to see the ball better against certain pitchers.

been able to take some heat off his fastball. I did the same with Mario Soto of Cincinnati in an All-Star game one year. Mario has great stuff—a superb fastball combined with a devastating change-up. Well, in my mind, it was important to close the miles-per-hour gap between his fastball and change, to make the pitches look more alike, reducing my chance of being fooled. (Nobody likes to look foolish, especially in an All-Star game.) So I went into my crouch. Mario obliged, bringing his fastball down, lowering its speed—and its effectiveness. That, in turn, made his change a bit easier to detect.

Now, I know what you're thinking. Will the umpire buy this move? Absolutely. If an ump notices you're dropping down— as long as it's not ridiculously low—he's going to compensate in his crouch and go down with you. If he doesn't, don't be shy; mention it to him between innings, anywhere out of earshot of the pitcher or catcher.

Fastball pitcher, three-quarter motion. Basically, most pitchers who throw at three-quarter sidearm make more pitches that end up down in the strike zone than up. It's just the nature of their delivery; most of their pitches tend to sink. In this case, my preference is to crouch a bit, to come down to the baseball.

Finally, I usually stand up straight in only two cases (this is how scientific one can get): against left-handers who come over the top and high-ball pitchers who don't have the "stuff" to overpower me up. Against lefties from the side, I crouch. My reasoning runs like this: Against over-the-top left-handers I'm a much better high-ball hitter, so I stay up. Lefties who come from the side give me trouble when I'm upright, so I drop down to get better visibility on the pitch.

And now a word or two about stance and slump. I think most hitters think that when they're in a slump they need a complete overhaul instead of looking carefully for a small cause. In my case, I leave my stance alone, getting a little more aggres-

This is my straight-up stance. I use it against a pitcher who pitches me high but doesn't have the velocity or movement on his pitch to overpower me there.

sive with my hands and, again, staying on the same plane as the ball. The stance is the base from which your entire game is built. Take your time finding the right one(s), but, when you do, stick with it (them).

Five

———— ◆ ————

CONTACT!

"Rod Carew influenced me a lot. Watching him use the whole field has helped make me the hitter I am today. He goes up there with a lot of different stances for different pitchers, but the bottom line on Rod Carew is he hits the ball where it's pitched."

Don Mattingly
1985 American League MVP

The analogy may seem a bit bizarre, but to become a dangerous presence at the plate, you need to add some music to your life. At times, the music must be hot, aggressive, as when the hands drive through the strike zone, attacking the baseball. Other times, as during the glide that sets up the swing, a softer, more delicate approach is necessary. Mess up this harmony—make a heavy-metal movement when easy-listening will do—and you'll find yourself hitting nothing but a lot of sour notes. Therefore, your goals as a hitter should be simple and direct. Make solid, consistently crisp contact. No excess movements, no complicated formulas. Just get the bat head into the proper position to drive through the contact zone.

The entire hitting process begins, quite naturally, when you step into the batter's box. Light music is suitable here. Don't make a big deal out of digging a hole for your back foot, or

This sequence of photos nicely illustrates my swing at work.

1

2

Photo 4
I've landed softly on my front toe, completing the movement toward the ball . . .
my weight is now evenly distributed . . .
my toe is slightly open to allow my hips to get through . . . my hands are still back and have not yet tightened on the bat.

Photo 5
Final approach into the ball . . . all my weight is now forward . . . my elbow is in tight to help me keep my hands back . . .
my hands finally tighten on the bat . . .
my head and eyes are on the ball.

Photo 6
Contact! . . . My hands are on the same plane as the ball and fully flat on extension
. . . my weight is on the outside of my front foot as that leg braces my swing . . . my hips release . . . my head stays on the ball.
. . . This pitch is going up the middle on a line drive.

4

Photo 1

My weight is back . . . my hands are softly on the bat . . . my front toe is raised off the ground to give me good leg flexibility . . . my eyes are trained on the pitcher.

Photo 2

My hands are churning downward as my swing is beginning . . . my weight is still back . . . my grip on the bat is still very loose . . . I'm beginning my stride.

Photo 3

My hands have made their way back up . . . my head is tucked as my weight is making a shift forward . . . my hands are still back, and loose on the bat.

pawing or smoothing the dirt. All you're doing is alerting the catcher to your exact location in the box. I try to cover up the holes that other guys left. I like a flat surface. I don't want my back foot, for example, lower than my right foot; then it's as if I'm hitting up a hill. So I settle in easily, inconspicuously. When you do decide where to stand (for me, it's the back-inside edge of the box), make sure you've got proper plate coverage; make sure your bat can reach pitches off the outside corner.

My front leg remains flexible, ready to open or close depending on the style of pitcher I'm facing. My weight is distributed onto my back leg, saving me the motion of rocking back as the pitcher begins his windup. I don't think you can hit effectively without first moving back before you move forward, so I just start back. My hands, at this point, are held about letter high, a foot or so from my body. I'm holding the bat loosely, free of tension. My bat at this point is almost parallel to the ground, very flat. My reason for keeping the bat flat and near the letters is strictly personal. It's a comfortable place to start. What you want to avoid, however, are the extremes: hands held stationary well above the shoulder, or down below the waist. Both contribute to increased, unnecessary movement and long, looping swings, which limit reaction time and ultimately rob you of proper arm extension.

What you're shooting for next is crucial to good hitting: a rhythmic glide into the ball; a balanced, streamlined weight shift; and an aggressive, hand-driven swing. You can't be stationary and expect to hit well; you lose too much flexibility and consistency. With this in mind, here's a step-by-step breakdown of one swing that's been a rather big hit over the years.

Step 1: The Setup

Watch the pitcher. Don't stare a hole through him, but remember what you've learned about focusing on the release point and reading the spin. As the pitcher begins to come out of his motion, your hands should begin to "churn." By that I mean

Each person has a dominant eye, one that is stronger than the other. Normally, right-handers are right-eye dominant, left-handers left-eye dominant. I'm lucky; I'm a left-handed hitter who is right-eye dominant, which means my dominant eye is closest to the pitcher. To find out which is your dominant eye, pick up a camera or a telescope. Which eye do you look through? That's your dominant eye.

they should drop downward, toward the waist, beginning your rhythm. Then bring them back up, taking your bat from its previous flat position into a 90-degree angle behind the head (a place, incidentally, at which many players begin their stroke). The reason I "churn" before a pitch is that it releases some tension and starts me into the rhythm of the one-piece swing. It is a pendulumlike effect. Swing down, swing up, never resting at any point in the arc. The eyes, in this situation, never leave the pitcher's hand; the head is tucked in tight, resting on the front shoulder. You want both eyes facing the pitcher, so turn your head—not too far—until you've gained full vision. Each person has a dominant eye—one eye that is stronger than the other. In most cases, right-handers are right-eye dominant and left-handers are left-eye dominant. The reason I bring this up is because in most cases, your weaker eye is the eye that's closest to the pitcher, and thus gets the first look at the ball. That is why it's important to get both eyes as square to the pitcher as possible. Bring that dominant eye into play as much as possible.

Now, as the pitcher is about to release the ball, remember: The bat should be in a ready position, near 11 o'clock, hands and weight back, front heel off the ground. Your back side (left side for lefty, right for righty) should remain vertical, near 90 degrees, not tilting at the waist.

Step 2: The Stride

The purposes of the stride are varied: It gets your energies moving in the right direction, eliminates a flat-footed swing, balances the weight shift, and decreases tension. So how do you find the right stride? As with so many other things, you experiment. We all tend to gravitate to what's comfortable, so keep that in mind during batting practice. Use different strides, short and long, and see what best suits your body type. For my money, a short stride (about 4 to 6 inches) is best; a longer stride generally limits your flexibility, has a tendency to pull

This three-photo sequence illustrates my stride. Although my front foot is open to begin with, my stride is still toward the pitcher. I land softly on the front toe to retain flexibility in my legs.

Whether your stance is opened or closed, your stride toward the ball is the key to keeping your body in a position to let you drive the ball.

your hands or torso too far forward, forcing you to lunge after the ball. Remember, you can make big strides as a hitter without *taking* them. Harmon Killebrew, a former teammate, did. He hit 573 career home runs (an average of 1 every 14 at-bats, fifth on the all-time percentage list), and Harmon, for a big man, had one of the shortest strides I've ever seen.

Now, once you decide on a stride, don't change it. You may decide, depending on the pitcher, to set up in different areas of the batter's box, but your stride should always be in the same direction—right back at the pitcher. And no matter what stance I take, the length of the stride never varies, and my front toe always faces on a 45-degree angle. With an angled front toe, you eliminate the tendency to open up too quickly with your hips, forcing your front shoulder to open and the head and eyes to follow. If you're doing your mechanics properly, the hips, shoulders, and head should open naturally, forcing your hands through the strike zone. By the time your front foot hits, the ball is halfway to home plate, and you will have made a decision on whether to swing or take the pitch. If you take it, just keep the hands back and follow the ball into the catcher's glove. But if you decide to swing, well, that's when your hands have to go to work.

Step 3: Flat-Hand Hitting

If any single idea dominates my approach to hitting, it would be my undying belief in the advantages of flat-hand hitting. The advantages are these: increased *flexibility* to react to a variety of pitches; more *leverage* in driving the baseball; better *arm extension*; ability to get the *bat and ball on the same plane*; a later, more natural *rolling of the wrists*; and the ability to *wait longer* on any pitch.

Flat-hand hitting is a term directly opposed to the often-taught method of top-hand hitting, or rolling your wrists as the ball and bat come together. Fundamentally, instead of having the fingertips of your top hand pointing to the sky—as they would

When you are a flat-hand hitter, the fingernails of your top hand will be pointing toward the sky as your bat passes through the contact zone. Flat hands will help you to get maximum extension of your arms.

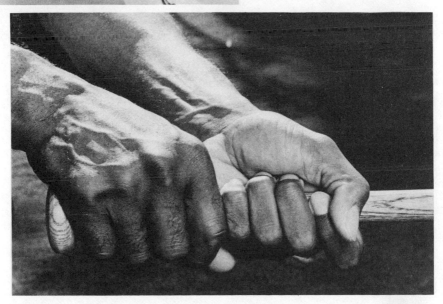

This is an example of top-hand hitting. Notice how the top thumb has rolled over as the bat passes the hitting zone. This causes a hitter to get tied up inside and subsequently to get no extension.

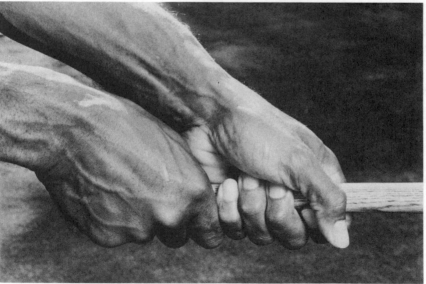

be if your hands were flat—your top-hand thumb is down, the fingertips either facing downward or pointed at the pitcher. But as you will see—and this is important—flat-hand hitting does not mean the bat never leaves a horizontal plane. On the contrary, *the angle of the bat adjusts with the location of the pitch. The location of the pitch, in turn, dictates when the hands are released.*

Your back elbow is a key to flat-hand hitting. It ignites the swing, flattening out your hands automatically as it presses down into your side. Try it. Stand up with an imaginary bat. Get your bat in the 11-o'clock position. Now pull down with your back elbow. The fingertips on the top hand should begin to point skyward, the bat moving, as you swing, toward horizontal.

You must remember that to become a threat at the plate, both hands must work for you. The bottom hand, in this sequence, works with the back elbow to pull the hands through the strike zone. The role of the top hand is most often to "quicken" the stroke, to help direct the bat head on the proper angle to the baseball. The back wrist in this flat-handed position remains cocked. Keeping it cocked forces your hands farther in front of the bat head, and on every pitch except those thrown inside, you want your hands to lead the swing. Okay, now we're in an optimum hitting position—back elbow in, hands flat, wrists cocked, head stationary, weight shifted, arms beginning to extend. What next? It all depends on the pitch.

Inside Pitch

Whether it's a fastball or an off-speed pitch, the basic stride-swing fundamentals don't change; only the release of the hands changes. By "release" I mean making a conscious decision to go after the pitch, to fire the bat at the ball. And I do mean fire. You can't baby your hands through the contact zone. Take a rip! Be aggressive. React. When a ball is bearing down inside, you want to commit your hands earlier than when the pitch is in the middle of the plate or outside. Doing so gets your hands, and thus the bat head, through the contact zone

These two photos are good examples of how little the swing changes on an inside pitch and an outside pitch. The obvious difference is my elbow. On the outside pitch, my elbow is farther away from the body, to let me get good arm extension. On the inside pitch, my elbow is in closer to my body, to help me keep my hands back and open my hips quicker.

Study my eyes. They are riveted on the ball. All you have to do is look at my eyes to know where the ball is.

sooner, allowing you to get your hips quickly into the swing. But don't get careless. Stay on balance and remain composed. And once that light inside your brain flashes the word "swing," be ready to explode at the baseball.

Now, at contact, the barrel of your bat should be, on the pitch inside, parallel with your hands. If you're doing things really right, the barrel should be beyond home plate.

Okay, so we know how and at what point to hit the ball. Now let's make sure we hit it. Ego is a strong emotional force, and it works for—and against—all of us in life. In baseball, we all want to hit home runs. Face it: We'd all love to be remembered as a Ruth, a Mantle, a Jackson, or a Murphy. Some say there's no bigger thrill than jogging around the bases, the crowd chanting your name. And, truth be told, it's hard to beat. But not all of us—in fact, very few of us—are born home-run hitters. We don't possess the size, the strength, or the raw power to play home-run derby successfully. I can't tell you how many times in my career I've seen a situation where a single would win a game and some big lug was up at the plate, swinging like there was no tomorrow.

It's the same sad song in Little League: so many big swings and so little contact, with style winning out over substance. So if you're consistently striking out or missing pitches, dial down a bit on the swing. Concentrate on contact.

Finally, imagine writing a symphony and forgetting the last movement. Like any artist, if you quit before you've finished—for us, before contact—you've stopped just short of success. Therefore, as a line-drive hitter, a gap hitter, it's crucial to remember to follow through upon contact, extending your arms and the bat head. It's the only way I know that we small guys can compete with the bigger hitters.

A Pitch over the Middle or Outside

The key here is to delay the wrist release in relation to how far the ball is from the middle of home plate. The farther outside the ball is, the longer you can wait. But the approach doesn't

Different strokes for different folks. These two pictures clearly illustrate the difference between a power hitter and a line-drive hitter. Reggie's swing has power ripping all through it. Look at his waist and upper body. Everything is cranked up. Look at mine. Everything is even and balanced. A Reggie Jackson can overpower a pitcher. A Rod Carew can't. That's why line-drive hitters must remember to follow through and get full extension of their arms and the bat head. It's the only way we can compete with the Reggie Jacksons.

differ: The wrists still move into the pitch in a cocked position, hands flat, back elbow pinching the body. Force yourself to wait, to delay committing to the ball, until the pitch has entered the contact zone. Often now, because of my practice and experience, I can wait until the pitch is just a few feet from home plate before I "fire" my hands at the ball, knowing that all the other mechanics are in place, the weight shifted, head steady.

With an outside pitch, your hands must get ahead of the bat head. The swing itself should look something like a hard "slap." You don't have to try to overpower the pitch; just concentrate on contact. You'll be shocked how quickly the ball travels into an infield hole or an outfield gap. And hit the ball where it's pitched; don't pull a pitch that has "opposite field" written all over it, or you'll wind up hitting weak ground balls.

Hitting the Breaking Ball
This is the bane of almost every hitter. The key to hitting the curve is deciding where the ball is headed and *being patient* enough to let it get there. The major difference in adjustment to inside and outside curves is in where the ball contacts the bat. The ideal contact point on the bat, whatever the pitch, is 2 to 2½ inches from the outside edge of the "trademark"—the spot on the bat where the manufacturer's logo is imprinted.

With breaking pitches, hand quickness is paramount—get the bat head on the ball!—and patience a virtue. Don't lunge after a pitch. Let it come to you. Then explode at the ball. The longer you can keep your hands back, your head still, and your body in balance, the better, more consistent contact you'll make. Remember: Let the ball come to you before you make your move.

Finally, I realize, fastball or curve, inside or out, your initial reaction, when thinking about rhythm, stride, and swing, will be to swing in steps: one . . . two . . . three. But hitting isn't square dancing, or field-goal kicking. You can't take the hands back . . . then step . . . then swing. It takes too much time; the result will be not instinctive or reactive but laborious and mechanical. You must strive for—and, believe me, it's not easy—three distinct movements meshed into one, the separate movements distinguishable perhaps to a slow-motion video camera but seen as a single component by the naked eye.

The Upper Half

What's going on upstairs, with the torso and shoulders, while our hands are working overtime? Ideally, not too much. The less movement the better; you don't want to disturb an otherwise balanced, rhythmic stride and swing. One important point, though: Remember to move your head *down* with the pitch. I can't emphasize enough the importance of eliminating excess head movement, of keeping that head down and tucked. Move it, and your shoulders pull out, and you lose critical balance and control.

Obviously, another benefit of keeping your head down is allowing you to "see" the bat hit the ball. But can you really see it? I don't think so. Sometimes, though, when you're really in the groove, it seems as though you can, even though closing your eyes upon contact is a natural, instinctive, involuntary reaction. What you have to do is work to keep your eyes open and on the ball as long as you can. One of the big problems with .250 hitters is that they may see the ball fine out of the hand, but they lose sight of the pitch over the last 3 feet. They're "57½-foot hitters," groping and guessing where the pitch is headed, an unfortunate situation because so much of the movement on a fastball, curve, or slider comes so late, often in those last 3 feet. You'll find the longer you keep your head down and your eyes open the better contact you'll make.

The Bottom Half

The truth is, the bottom part of your body—the legs and hips—is the better half when it comes to hitting a baseball. Unfortunately, many players—particularly young ones—neglect it. Yes,

Always follow the ball, even if you are going to take the pitch. Do this for two reasons: as a way to discipline yourself to keep your head down and your eye on the ball and so you can gauge the umpire's strike zone.

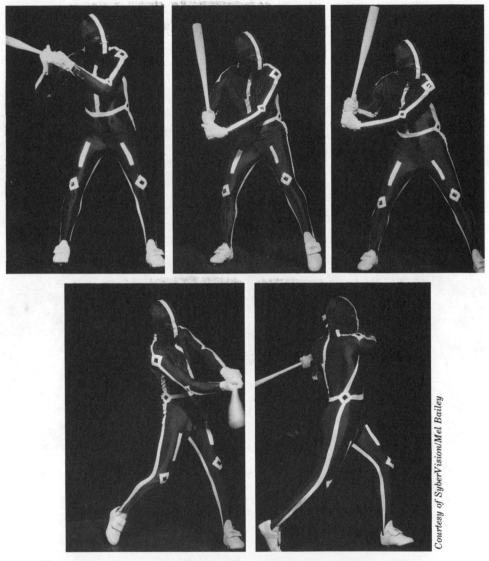

This is how my swing would look if I were a right-handed hitter. The special effects illustrate how little movement there is in my swing. Everything stays in place until I make my final approach into the ball. Notice how all the markings line up. My body is under control throughout the swing.

I can see you in the weight rooms now, muscling up on the machines, thinking the bigger you are upstairs the better hitter you'll be. Not so. True, muscles and strength are important, but get too pumped up and you'll find your fluid stride, your rhythm, all out of sync, unable to produce the long ball—more than likely the reason you starting lifting weights in the first place. Instead, concentrate on good mechanics and a quick swing and you'll find yourself driving the ball, no matter what your size.

But back to the bottom half. In every swing, it's important that your body stay squarely balanced, turning tightly, as if a pole were running from the top of your cap through the middle of your body and you rotated on this axis. The hips should open naturally with the swing, the rotation squarely in the direction of the pitcher. What you want to guard against—and this is something all players fall prey to from time to time—is opening up too soon. This causes an immediate chain reaction, pulling out your front shoulder, taking your torso, arms, head, and everything else imaginable off the ball. What remains is a leaning tower, unbalanced, useless. And what about the back leg? Here are two points: When contact is made, the back leg, from the foot to the hip, should be angled with the toes turned toward the pitcher. The heel is up off the ground. This movement facilitates proper hip rotation; it keeps the entire body in one tight, vertical alignment, a prerequisite to a powerful stroke.

To Uppercut or Not to Uppercut

Because the baseball generally comes to home plate on a downward path, many hitters feel compelled to compensate by swinging up on the baseball to "level out" the pitch. Not me. Uppercutting has really only one place in my baseball book: when your team needs a sacrifice fly and you must lift the ball to the outfield. In that case, it's okay to uppercut certain pitches. Otherwise, I don't believe in it. Here's why: It's very likely

This is an example of an uppercut swing. Notice how my entire left side has collapsed. This causes my right shoulder and hips to fly open and will result in my getting under the ball. Uppercut swings are better left for players like Reggie, the great power hitters whose job it is to beat you with one swing.

most of your hits will be airborne, and lofted fly balls make the easiest outs. Also, uppercutting creates difficulty in getting the arms fully extended and your weight properly transferred— keys to solid contact. Even more important, it causes the collapse of the rear leg and shoulder, which, in turn, causes the batter to tilt backward, raising the front shoulder and opening the front hip too early. It also brings the hands and bat down to an ineffective position.

When a person suffers from uppercutting, the reason is usually an improper weight shift—that is, not getting the weight shifted from the back foot to the front foot. As I said, you need to move your weight forward when you stride. By taking the weight off the back leg and transferring it forward, you'll cure any problems associated with uppercutting. Of course, not every pitch is perfect, every fastball belt high, every swing level. Consequently, as hitters, we must be able to adjust to pitches that are a shade too high or too low, ones that require us occasionally to take imperfect cuts. But if we are going to err, it's best to make a mistake of hitting down on a ball rather than up. At least with ground balls, you're giving yourself half a chance. With the advent of artificial turf, with dirt infields known for a bad hop or two, and given the fact that fielders must first catch and then throw the baseball, ground balls simply make for tougher plays. I have a similar theory for "dead pull" hitters. I'm not against pulling the ball. If you have the ability, fine. But what I've found is that by pulling every ball, you narrow your hitting area by one half or more. You also get into situations against pitchers you have no business trying to pull.

Avoiding Infield Pop-Ups

Toward the latter part of 1985, Wade Boggs of the Red Sox received some well-deserved national attention. For the most part, it focused on the fact that he had finished the season with 240 hits, one more than I had in 1977, which, until Boggs surpassed it, was the most by any hitter since 1930. The statistic, however, that caught many an eye was this: Boggs went almost the entire season (until September) before he popped out to the infield. Well, I don't know if that stat has ever been kept on me, but I doubt that I've popped out to an infielder fifty times in twenty years, and, as with Boggs, there are several reasons. First of all, we're not very interested in hitting the bottom half of the baseball. We'll consciously try to hit the middle half or the top half, and we also have the discipline to lay off high or rising pitches that are made for popping up.

Additionally, Boggs and I don't uppercut on the ball unless, as I've said, we are in a situation that calls for us to hit a sacrifice fly to the outfield. That's one reason you like to have Reggie Jackson at the plate if you need a fly ball. Reggie's stroke is an uppercut swing that's primed for power. Reggie hits a lot of long fly balls, but he also pops up to the infield quite a bit. That's one of the benefits of flat-hand hitting. It acts as a deterrent to hitting pop flies to the infield, because by the sheer mechanics of the swing it forces you to use the whole bat, keeping it steady as you drive through the baseball. In top-hand hitting, you are rolling the bat in a downward motion, thus exposing the top half of the bat, in effect, compounding the problem of making contact because the bat is moving not only forward but downward. Even with a level arm movement, unless you hit the ball perfectly, you're most likely going to pop the ball up, pull it foul, or miss it entirely.

What also causes pop-ups to the infield is waiting too long to pull the trigger—not exploding at a pitch you want to hit. Through indecisiveness, a hitter can "jam" himself with a pitch—unlike a "jam" imposed by a pitcher throwing inside. If you wait until the ball is too deep in the contact zone, you're going to get jammed and never get the barrel of the bat on the ball. If you are fortunate to make contact on the narrow part of the bat, there just isn't enough wood there to get the ball into the outfield.

Up the Middle/Opposite Field

The best way to earn respect as a hitter is to learn to hit the ball up the middle. I know, I know: easier said than done. I realize that most of you are not professionals, and that in Little League or high school, practices are brief and attention spans short. There are more pressing priorities than hitting 200 balls right back at the pitcher. But there's really only one way that's going to change, and that's with practice. Hard, sweaty, serious practice. Eventually that practice will pay off, just as it did for me in the third inning on August 4, 1985. I was facing Frank Viola of Minnesota and was one hit shy of becoming only the sixteenth man in baseball history to record 3,000 career hits. At 1:47 p.m., Viola threw a 1-1 slider, and I flared a soft line drive into short left field. Afterward, my teammate Bob Boone mentioned how appropriate the location of that historic hit was. "It wouldn't have been right had it been any other type of hit," he said. The implication was obvious: Of my 3,000-plus career hits, hundreds have been into what I call My Favorite Spot.

And just exactly where is this garden spot? For a left-handed hitter, it's a large area that starts about five feet to the hitter's right of second base and extends all the way to the left-field line. For a righty, the area shifts from just to the left of second base to the right-field line. And why is it so rewarding? Well, up the middle/opposite field is nice because it allows for mistakes, for miscalculations. If you're a lefty, say, and always aiming for that spot (except in specific situations, which we'll discuss in Chapter Eight), and on a given pitch you're off a bit, the ball can still fall in front of the center fielder or left fielder, skip past the shortstop, go over second base, or bounce off the pitcher for a hit. So remember this phrase: up the middle/opposite field. Recite it. Burn it inside your head. Learn to contact the ball and drive it there (with adjustments, of course, for inside pitches), and you'll go a long way as a hitter.

Six

♦

THE MENTAL GAME

So much of baseball is played inside the head. It's a silent fight, waged not before a crowd, in public view, but rather in darkness, in hotel rooms or locker rooms, a battle between the forces of self-doubt and dogged determination. And it is the losers of those battles who so often speak of a lack of confidence, an innate fear of playing under pressure.

There are, in my mind, two kinds of confidence that affect performance at the plate. The first kind deals with the ability to overcome outside influences, having a strong enough character to deal with negative press, overbearing fans and coaches—you name it. The other, more subtle type of confidence deals with how *you* perceive yourself as a player. Do *you* believe you're a starter or a bench warmer? Do *you* believe you're an all-star or an also-ran? If the answers to these questions are the latter, your play on the field will reflect it. But when you've learned to shut off outside influences and believe in yourself, there's no telling how good a player you can be. That's because you've got the mental edge. When you have that edge, when you feel it, no pitcher is too tough, no worry worth sweating. Lose it, however, and see how quickly the game changes. Hits stop falling. Worries increase. Excuses multiply. The lesson is, if you don't have confidence in yourself as a hitter, if you don't believe you're good, no book on hitting will make a difference.

First, let's take a look at overcoming outside influences, the most common—yet easiest—problems to control. I always advocate making rational decisions before taking any action. Don't do anything rash. Seek counsel from a coach, a parent, a pastor—don't let it burn inside you. Remember, you're going to have bad days. You're going to make errors. People are going to boo. Don't compound the problem by making obscene gestures or tasteless remarks. As soon as you give credence to outside influences, the situation only gets worse. So walk away and let your bat and glove do the talking. Of course—and I say this cautiously—there does come a time when you have to make a stand and fight for what's right. Just think before acting— that's all.

I found out about booing first-hand in 1974 when I led the league in errors at second base, with 33. I can't count the number of times I wanted to crawl under the bag and disappear. Often my frustrations over being unmercifully booed—even though I was hitting well—spilled out in the locker room. One day it caught up with me. After a particularly difficult day I said something like, "Man, it sure would be nice to have a change." That, in turn, was twisted by a newspaperman into a trade request that read in the paper "Carew Wants to Be Traded." So be careful. The press are very positive and well-meaning most of the time, but, face it, you've got to be careful about what comes out of your mouth.

Pressures

In 1985 I experienced more outside pressure than most players feel in a lifetime. The pressure of becoming only the sixteenth player in history to record 3,000 hits was frightening, particularly because of the growing specter of a players' strike. I didn't want to wait until it was settled to pursue the milestone, because, in truth, the way things looked for a time, I didn't know if it would ever be settled.

So, this time, I learned from my experiences in 1977, the

year I almost hit .400 (I finished at .388). That year, no matter where I went, the scene never varied: tape recorders in the face, phone calls at the hotel. We had to change our telephone number every two weeks. And always the same questions over and over: "Are you going to hit .400?" "What are you doing differently?" "Why are you hitting so well?"

I learned then I shouldn't allow myself to go through that grind again. I decided that even though 3,000 hits was a major milestone, I was going to shut myself off from reporters, do what I had to do, because in '77 the pressure had affected not only my fielding but my baserunning, my concentration, everything. I know that sounds like a harsh decision, and certainly among the press it was an unpopular one. Celebrity is wonderful, but without on-field performance, you have no claim to celebrity.

Now, how does pressure reach down from the major-league level into college, high school, even Little League? Easily. We all want to start, to make All-Star teams, to please our coaches, parents, scouts. But first we have to please ourselves. We have to feel good about the effort, have the confidence that if given the opportunity, we'll perform.

So, work and learn to believe in yourself, even if you don't get that precious college scholarship. Get a job; try out; find some way to play ball, if that's what is important to you. Whether or not you get that scholarship is not entirely in your hands. During my high-school years, at George Washington in the Bronx, I played sandlot baseball in the Bronx Federation League, a tough, well-scouted circuit. One day, the director of the Minnesota Twins farm system came to see me play. Was I nervous! This was my big chance. But you have to settle down. If scouts are in the stands, forget them; keep your mind on the game and concentrate on doing the little things right, being sound fundamentally. Use two hands during warmups; hustle. Give off a glow that says "I love this game." And be careful how you dress. Personally, I'm a neatnik; my uniform has to be clean at all times. If it gets dirty, I change it. You, however, may have your own style of play, more Charlie Hustle, more down and dirty than me. That's fine. But don't look sloppy. A dirty uniform is one thing; a shirttail hanging out, silly hats during pregame warmups, droopy pants, quite another. Scouts have a sixth sense about this attitude; so, clean or dirty, play like you mean it. By the way, the day the scout came to see me, we were playing on a field adjacent to Yankee Stadium. I was 9 for 10 in a doubleheader and hit 4 home runs.

Still, with all this effort, I'm a big believer in balancing the scales, in cultivating off-field hobbies and interests to draw your mind away from these pressures. You can't think baseball, football, whatever, twenty-four hours a day. You need a private life, a release. And if you're still in school, you need to know the books come first. You need a safety net, career opportunities, in case for whatever reason you don't make it to the big leagues. After all, how many players do? And don't be blinded by hero worship. To me it's great to have young kids look up to athletes, movie stars, famous people, but take a look in another direction once in a while—to the head of your class, to your teachers.

Finally, unfortunately, you'll find as you get older that time just naturally becomes your enemy. When I was younger, in my teens and early twenties, my confidence soared; I knew I could hit. But at forty I realize now my days of .400 hitting are over; I'm not going to average .354 for six seasons anymore, as I did from 1973 through 1978. Father Time is fighting back. But still, I've learned to live with him and adjust, not to try to play beyond my abilities, not to attack pitches at forty the same way I did at twenty. In short, I've leaned to play within my limitations, whatever they may be.

One question often asked is "What happens if I'm drafted by the pros?" My advice, unless the money is extraordinary, is to go to college. If you're smart and have the desire for a life after baseball, get your degree. Quite honestly, college baseball today is just like a good minor-league experience—great coaching, travel, a "World Series" possibility, and 100-game schedules.

If you're good enough to start at that level, don't worry; you'll get your chance to become a professional.

The second form of confidence is more difficult to develop. Of course, some people are seemingly born with a special gleam in their eye, a swagger to their step: Pete Rose, Dwight Gooden, Dan Mattingly, Al Kaline, Tony Oliva. For others, the mental edge is gained slowly; bit by bit, they grow into their greatness. Growing up, I *knew* I was going to be a good hitter. I woke up every morning telling myself, "You're the best there is." Don't be afraid to say it, to *believe* it. If you don't, nobody else will.

Certainly, part of this confidence quotient comes from knowing the game, knowing that a pitcher tends to tire in the sixth inning, or that a certain outfielder's arm is weak. Putting this knowledge together with their superior skills has helped players like Rose and Oliva win many a ballgame. Knowing they had an edge gave them the confidence to take advantage of it.

The mental edge is not something you can buy or are born with. It begins long before you step into the batter's box. As I said, it means eating right, using the right equipment, knowing what you want to do at the plate with each pitcher you face. But it's also an attitude. A pitcher-be-damned, "I'm the best hitter you're going to face today or any other day" frame of mind that begins before you ever walk up to the plate. An attitude that says "You've got a load on your hands, buddy, and the last name is Carew," one that stems from the simple phrase "I'm going to get a hit." Every time I walk up to home plate, no matter what happened previously, whether I'm 0 for 20 or 5 for 5, I am going to get a hit. If I go up to home plate the first three times and get three singles, I want four singles. I'm never complacent. I never say, "Ah, what the heck; I've got four; who needs five?" *I* need five. And so do you. But with this confidence must also come discipline. Not the discipline espoused by Ted Williams, who said, "If you want to hit .300, you can only attack certain balls in certain zones." I've made a living hitting balls out of the strike zone; in fact, I've hit far more pitches out of the strike zone than down the middle. Nowadays, when I see a fastball at the letters, I do a double-take. "What's this guy doing?" I ask myself. So, if you think you can handle a so-called ball, take a rip, especially if you know exactly what you want to do with that pitch. Some guys don't, but swing anyway, compounding the problem by taking a mediocre pass at a somewhat bad pitch.

Still, so much has to do with what you *think* you can do, which directly relates to how you feel at the plate. In my mind, I'm in complete control in the box: composed, confident, quiet, concentrating on nothing but the task at hand. I put no outside pressure on myself—and that means, no matter how difficult it may be, not permitting personal problems to color my thinking. Unfortunately, this is easier said than done. Today, a lot of major-league hitters walk up to home plate worrying about everything but hitting. Their contract. Their girlfriend. Their error in the previous inning. The game's too tough for a distracted effort. If you bring outside pressures between the white lines, you're adding to your miseries. You almost have to be a machine out there, turned on when you come to the park, playing on something akin to automatic pilot. *You can get a hit anytime you want to and you're going to get a hit.*

For you, the lesson to be learned and memorized, especially in youth, is not to compromise. Don't accept failure on *any* pitch. One player—young, very talented—succumbed for a short time. He'd sit on the bench befuddled, time and time again, by fastballs fed one after another on the outside of the plate. So what did he do? The worst possible thing. He started inching in, moving closer to the plate. Well, the next thing he knows, here comes the hard stuff—on the *inside* corner. So now he backs off. So they go back outside. Now he's *really* talking to himself.

If this player had practiced hitting the outside fastball over the course of a week or two weeks, he would have put a stop to the problem. At the very least, he would have seen hundreds of pitches in that trouble spot, and this would have helped him recognize the pitch, speed his reflexes, focus his attention on improving his hand-eye coordination. It took him a while, but that's what he finally did. So should you. Use a tee. Just set it up on the outside corner of the plate. Then concentrate, as if in a game, on every swing. You won't have to wait long to see the results.

Another common mental problem is how to handle a guy who always seems to have your number. No matter what you do, you can't seem to get a hit. I had that problem for years with Rudy May, the former New York Yankee left-hander. He *owned* me, principally because his motion (all arms and legs) was very confusing to me. My theory in this situation has always been to check my mechanics. I wasn't seeing the ball well, and I figured I had to make a mechanical adjustment. Well, I experimented for years—and I do mean years—without success. Finally, Rudy retired. Thank goodness! When this happens to you, your first adjustment should always be to run a mechanical check, opening your stance, closing it, waiting longer to take the outside pitch to right or left. The second adjustment is mental. You cannot say to yourself, "This pitcher is better than I am." Because as a hitter, *no* pitcher is better than you. *Nobody*. As soon as you give in to Mr. A, you'll find it easier to concede an at-bat to Mr. B, then Mr. C. Pretty soon there's nobody left in the alphabet.

Slumps

Slumps are funny in how they can turn an otherwise well-adjusted human being into a frustrated, tentative creature. I've seen slumps make a perennial All-Star selection change his stance every day. This player figured he could change his fundamental approach to a very difficult task and expect to get in a groove. Well, it didn't work. It can't work.

Slumps are a part of the game, as indigenous to baseball as the national anthem and hot dogs. Play long enough and you'll stop hitting for a spell. What differentiates the better players from the rest is how they cope with temporary failure, no matter how exceedingly frustrating it is. Anybody who has played the game knows what I'm going to say. Hit a shot—a bullet—right at somebody, watch him catch it, and see how it feels. Or watch some infielder or outfielder pull a play out of his pants. My remedy for slumps is rather tried but still very true: a visit to the batting cage. But only a short visit—ten or fifteen minutes a day. That's it. Work on what you want to work on, and get out. If you stay longer, you get sore, or lazy, falling right back into your bad habits.

Also, don't attempt any major overhauls when a little fine-tuning will do. I think changing everything is the worst possible decision, especially if you're hitting in poor luck. If, however, you're continually popping pitches up, or, worse, missing them, go to the videotape (they're the best way to detect mistakes) or have a *knowledgeable* coach watch your swing. You may be pulling off the ball; maybe your hands are lazy; maybe your back leg and shoulder are collapsing; but if you—via videotape—or a manager, coach, or teammate can spot these problems, all the better. Again, beware. Some managers have a good eye for hitting. Others do not. And though I think it's a coach's or teammate's duty to try to help, make sure that person has some track record or at least can speak intelligently about hitting. It's the same for you. If you see a teammate doing something new in the box, mention it. Don't belabor the point, but bring it up. I've had coaches who have seen me hit for years spot a tiny flaw, a new wrinkle in my swing. The next day I'm in the cage trying to iron it out. Also, coaches, teammates, offer some encouragement! If a guy in a slump hits a shot, speak up. A "good hit" or "nice stroke" goes a long way in boosting someone's sagging ego.

Another problem associated with a trip to rock bottom is a player's tendency to try to blast his way out of a slump. What's wrong with a bunt or two? Psychologically, it's a blessing, hitting a ball thirty feet for a single when dozens of long flies have been caught. Bunting is not something I'd try during a hot streak, when you should stay aggressive and swing away as much as possible. But during a downturn, when your confidence is hurting, a bunt is a perfect tonic.

Ultimately, though, slumping comes down to a state of mind. Let it eat at you and, many times, there'll be nothing left. This is where confidence *and* discipline really come to bat. You must discipline yourself to abide by the ten keys to good hitting, to relax and try not to force it, to remain confident in your abilities—even if no one else is.

Seven

◆

THE CONFRONTATION

Like it or not, boiled down to its lowest common denominator, baseball is a numbers game. As a player, you are constantly judged by the number of hits, runs, and RBIs you accumulate, how you fare in what can be called "the confrontation." This individual battle between the pitcher and hitter occurs dozens of times each game; it's the heartbeat of any baseball game, and to improve you must acknowledge the importance of being mentally prepared for this confrontation. To help you, I've chosen two of my at-bats from one game in 1985, one-on-one duels with Seattle right-handers Jim Beattie and Karl Best. I hope that by analyzing these two at-bats pitch by pitch, thought by thought, you'll get a better understanding of what goes on inside my head. That should help you deal with your own confrontations, no matter on what level you play.

Friday, August 26, 1985, California vs. Seattle

Situation: Second inning. Runners on first and second, no outs. Angels have scored two runs and lead 3-1. Beattie, 6'7", 205, an eight-year major-league veteran, is on the mound facing Gary Pettis. Count is 1-2. Carew on deck.

Carew: In this case, I'm thinking that Gary should be looking to make contact and get at least one of the two runners into scoring position. That way, with a sacrifice fly or a hit we can get another run in, or keep the rally going. Gary is a tough player to double up because of his speed, so almost anything on the ground will move up the runners.

Action: Pettis takes a called third strike.

Carew: Beattie threw Gary a fastball in on his hands, a tough pitch, one Gary will learn to spoil (hit foul) as he gets more experience. I credit Beattie here. He made a great pitch.

As I move into the batter's box, I'm retracing my past against this pitcher. After eight years of battles, I know what his ball does, how he likes to pitch me. I realize a 3-1 lead this early in the game means nothing, but I know another base hit means one more run, some breathing room for our ballclub. So I'm looking base hit all the way. I'm not looking to move the runners over at this point. Not with one out. We've got Seattle on the ropes, one good shot away from a knockout. And I want to throw a big punch.

As I step into the box, smoothing out the dirt, planting my foot, I flash on my .400 average lifetime against Beattie. I'm 0-1 so far tonight, but he didn't do anything different my first time up from what he has done in previous years. "Pick up the ball," I tell myself. "Put it in play." I'm after a pitch I can drive; I'm not interested in going fishing, chasing sliders or sinkers. I know that Beattie has a tendency to get his fastball up, so I'm standing a bit more upright now, getting on a plane I feel the ball will be arriving on.

Action: Fastball in. Strike one called. 0-1.

Carew: Good pitch. He threw me a fastball that started on the inside edge and came back over the plate. It's the type of pitch I know from past experience ties me up, so, this being the first pitch, I take it rather than swinging and grounding out weakly to second or short. Now, with an 0-1 count, my thinking doesn't really change. I'm still looking for *my* pitch. I don't feel I'm behind; I treat it just like 0-0. I'm still looking for something I can get full arm extension on, something to drive to the opposite field. I want to drive that runner on second home.

Action: Fastball inside. Ball one. 1-1.

Carew: As I picked up that pitch right out of Beattie's hand, I knew it was a pitch to take. It seems that Beattie, or his catcher, or his coaching staff has decided to pitch me with fastballs in, jamming me so I can't extend my arms. I file that away. Now, after two inside fastballs, I'm thinking outside. Yet I'm ready just in case Beattie tries to slip something past me inside.

I settle back in. Beattie sees this and steps off the rubber. So I step out, relaxing. "He's trying to get himself under control," I think to myself. So I did the same.

He's back on the rubber now but still taking his time. I step out again. A lot of times, when a pitcher displays this much indecision, he's either confused about pitch selection or trying to break up your timing and concentration. You can't let that happen. That's why I stepped out. I'm letting Beattie know *I'm* in control of this confrontation. I'm making him wait for me, to pitch to me on my terms, on my schedule. It's easier to step out and start the process all over again than it is to try to set any endurance records.

I step back in. More trouble. Beattie's veteran catcher, Bob Kearney, calls time-out. Now I know something's up. It's possible that they can't decide what pitch to throw, but, more important, I think Kearney senses Beattie is struggling. I know from checking out Beattie's statistics that he finishes only about one of every six games he starts; he knows the game is on the verge of getting out of hand. This next pitch has to be his pitch;

he knows he can't make a mistake. This puts me at a decided advantage because this pitch is more important to him than to me. He doesn't want to get behind in the count; I'm perfectly comfortable hitting with two strikes, especially in a game where we're already two runs up.

Action: Sinker away. Ball two. 2-1.

Carew: A tempting offer, but I'm not in the mood to go fishing. I see the movement of the ball early and quickly decide it's nothing I'd be interested in. I thought he might go outside and he did, but it cost him because he missed, if only by a couple of inches. Now I'm up 2-1 and in the driver's seat. In this situation you want to be very selective. This is one of the best possible counts for any hitter (2-0 being the best). Now, if you get the pitch or location you want, let 'er rip. You can always pass on a pitch that ties you up or surprises you. In this case, be very selective of the pitches you'll swing at. If they're not in the very precise area you want them to be in, "spit on it," as we say in the majors: Take a look, and let it pass. There's plenty more to come.

Action: Fastball. Up, a little out, but over the plate.

Carew: This is the pitch Beattie has thrown me for years. It's also one of the reasons I'm hitting .400-plus lifetime against him. It's a pitch I've taken to left field hundreds of times in my career, and this time it's no different. As soon as he releases the ball, I know it's my pitch all the way. I remain patient, waiting, striding, wrists cocked, then explode at the pitch as it reaches the outside edge of the contact zone. Releasing my hands, I see the ball traveling to left-center; I've hit it well; it's slicing away from the center fielder, Phil Bradley, who has been playing me a little shallow. I know it's a double all the way. Standing on second base, that familiar inner glow comes over me. I've done my job. I knocked in a run, kept the rally going. I feel even better when the next hitter, Juan Beniquez, hits a three-run homer to put us ahead 7-1.

Situation: Same game, fifth inning, no outs, runners at first and second, reliever Best (6'4", 215) now pitching. This is his first full season in the league. Score still 7-1 Angels.

Carew: In the on-deck circle I'm thinking once again Gary (Pettis) has to get the runners over. We're in position to put this game totally out of sight, but Gary has to do his job.

Action: Pettis grounds to the right side, advancing the runners to second and third.

Carew: Nice job, Gary. A base hit here and this game is over. I haven't hit against Best too much, a couple of times in spring training, and earlier, in the third inning, when he walked me on a 3-1 count. I know from past experience he's very strong, has trouble throwing his breaking ball for strikes so he throws mostly fastballs—the prototypical short reliever, a carbon-copy of Beattie. I won't alter my batting stance too much.

But, to be honest, I'm not expecting Seattle to pitch to me. First base is open, there's one out, and Beniquez, a right-hander, is on deck. Best looks like he can be tough on righties, and Juan doesn't have the best running speed, so the situation is ripe for a double play if they put me on intentionally.

I step into the box, again making sure I'm set. Looking up, I notice the infield is drawn in. And Kearney's giving a sign. They're going to pitch to me—with the infield in, no less! Somebody hasn't done his homework. In 1984 I got the runner home from third base with less than two outs almost 80 percent of the time (11 out of 14 attempts). Now, to make matters worse (for them), they've brought the infield in, making me a .500 hitter. All I have to do is hit the ball hard on the ground, especially on artificial turf, and it's going to be a run. I can't believe they're pitching to me. Oh, well, their mistake. Best winds, delivers . . .

Action: Fastball, high and tight. Ball one.

Carew: He brushed me back. I'm not happy and shoot Best
a stare. You're either going to pitch to me or walk me, but
don't go throwing the ball under my chin. Go with your best
stuff. Don't play with me in this situation. The stare says, "You
can't intimidate me, pal." Now I'm even more determined to
get him. I have at times hit a ball hard and right back at a
pitcher when I've been unnecessarily thrown at, but this is not
the time for it. I can hurt him more by making sure I get the
runs home. I make a minor adjustment in my stance, coiling a
little to make sure I keep my front shoulder in.

Action: Slider inside, fouled off to the left side. Count is 1-1.

Carew: Pretty good pitch by Best, hard slider that jammed
me inside. I opened up a bit too quickly, pulling off the ball and
fouling it away. I was trying to go to the opposite field and
knew I didn't have the right mechanics on the swing, but my
hand action allowed me to keep the ball in foul territory. Now
I'm thinking I need to look for a pitch that I can take a better
cut at. I'm also aware that Best has made his first two pitches
inside to me, as Beattie did in the second.
    Catchers fall into patterns, too. After two pitches in the sec-
ond inning, Beattie went outside. The chances are good that
Kearney will call for an outside pitch, but again I'll stay flexible
enough in my thinking and mechanics to handle an inside pitch
if one is offered.

Action: Fastball in.

Carew: As soon as I see the ball, I know it's a pitch to hit.
The seams are spinning back toward the pitcher: I know it's a
fastball and that it's going to be inside. It's a pitch I can drive
into left or right, but instead of turning on the pitch, running
the risk of grounding out to second, I keep my hands back and,

at the last moment, let them explode into the ball, making sweet, solid contact to left-center.

Bradley is still playing shallow, and again I know this is a two-base hit. The ball takes one hop and goes into the stands for a ground-rule double. We're ahead 9-1 now, and this game is over. I've knocked in three runs, scored a fourth, and feel pretty good. But I'm not quite done. On second base I still have some unfinished business. I stare at Best until he sees me. After that brushback, I wanted to make sure he *saw* me standing on second, that he knew I was there because he didn't do his job. A subtle psych job but effective nonetheless. Can't let these kids get too cocky.

After the game, I review in my mind every pitch and every situation of that night's ballgame. One thing is consistently clear: Seattle is going to try to attack me inside this year. It's a pattern that does hold up throughout the remainder of the year, and, thanks in part to the input gained in this game, I go on to have a very good 1985 against the Mariners.

Well, now that we've put Beattie and Best to rest there are some other situations we didn't touch upon during those two showdowns. You'll need to know how to handle them, so here goes. The count is:

0-2. This time you have to forget about location, pitch, everything. Just find the ball as quickly as possible and attack it, letting your reflexes take over. In many cases, it can be easier to hit when behind 0-2 than at 0-1 because your concentration level naturally rises. The secret is not to get rattled and start guessing, or fishing for anything. If you can't get a pitch to drive, try to foul a good pitch off. To do this, wait as long as possible before committing.

3-0. An automatic take unless the "hit" sign is flashed by your coach or manager. Don't try to be a hero. Play by the rules. If you get the take sign, take the pitch. Don't be messing around, dropping your body or bat into the strike zone. If you do get the "green light," however, use some discipline. Most times the power hitters will be given the hit-away sign, simply because with one swing they can produce big results. But if you do get the go-ahead, power or not, make sure you reduce your strike zone. The pitch *must* be in your sweetest spot, or you're taking. You're too far ahead in the count to hit anything but a prime pitch. And don't be foolish and try to put one out of the park. Just take your regular cut, focusing in on the target spot. This way you'll get a full and aggressive swing.

3-1. Another great time for selective hitting. Don't chase. Have confidence that you can make solid contact with two strikes. Your own strike zone remains much the same as at 3-0, eyeing a pitch either down the middle or to your strengths.

3-2. No real edge here. Can't just look fastball, not these days, so watch for the baseball. Think release point. Hit the ball where it's pitched. Don't look location. Just look for the baseball and adjust accordingly.

Eight

SITUATIONAL HITTING

"Rod Carew is a great hitter because he is an unselfish hitter."

Don Baylor
1979 American League MVP

Baseball is nothing if not a game of situations. Bunt, bunt-and-run, hit-and-run, sacrifice fly, pinch-hitting, designated hitting. They all combine to make baseball a game within a game, a chess match played out in cleats. Players are often remembered (or forgotten) for their ability (or inability) to produce in situation baseball. Did he move the runner over when necessary? Could he hit the sacrifice fly? Was he a clutch player off the bench? Could he be counted on to deliver a big single when it mattered? All of these attributes go into being called a "team" or "clutch" player, revered words in any sport. But such respect from your peers doesn't come easily. You have to earn it, prove it, on the field, every day, day in and day out.

How do you become a top situational hitter? By etching two words into your mind: confidence and selection. You have to *believe* you can move a runner over or deliver the key sacrifice fly. You need a cocksure confidence, one I believe stems from study, observation, and conversation with players and coaches. It's the only way to learn what pitches to expect in certain situations. You must also develop a keen awareness of the count, what pitches you can expect at 2-1, 2-0, 1-2. Then you must learn to be ready mentally; preparation can, and often does, make the difference between a ground ball to second with a runner on third and a sacrifice fly to the outfield that scores a run.

One of the problems associated with situational hitting is, quite frankly, that some hitters don't enjoy the situations, the pressure, or the thought of giving up an at-bat. Players today, with their incentive-filled contracts and bonuses, have become very stat-minded, very individualistic in their approach to the game. For many, all they think of is, "Well, it's a sure out and my average is going to drop." Nice attitude. What they're really thinking is, "Sure, I can move the guy over, but maybe I can get a base hit, score the run, and be the hero," or "I'll go to the right side, but I'm not grounding out. I'm driving that ball between first and second." Or "I can hit a homer off this guy; I'm taking the first good pitch downtown." (The last two comments are usually followed by a pop-up to the infield or a strikeout.)

It's hard to believe, but many major-league ballplayers are oblivious of game situations, how the game evolves, the chess match between managers, particularly in late innings. They haven't been schooled enough to think ahead, to organize their attack. Consequently, when they are called upon, they quickly appear lost, for safety's sake reverting back to the ever-popular "get a hit" mentality—a strategy that brings pleasure to any pitcher's heart, a strategy I suggest has no place in this or any other sport.

Therefore, when you step up to the plate in a given situation, you have to be totally aware, tuned in to your job. If that means making an out to help the team win, so be it. No player's batting average is more important than the team's winning percentage. Your mind must be focused: Get the job done. That was one of the greatest things about Frank Robinson as a hitter. Some of his prettiest swings came while moving a hitter over from first to second.

In situational hitting, a single, universal premise applies: Look for *the* pitch that will allow you to accomplish the task at hand. Wait until you get that pitch, at least until you have two strikes.

Finally, before discussing specific situations, I want to reiterate one point made in Chapter Five. Unless a situation dictates otherwise, as a hitter you're concentrating on "up the middle/opposite field," adjusting your stroke to the location of the pitch. In short, staying within yourself, fighting the tendency to pull every pitch.

Situation 1: Advancing the Baserunner

One of the most common—but bedeviling—situations in the game. The object seems simple: Hit the ball on the ground to the right side, moving the runner into scoring position. It becomes even more important when moving a runner from second to third, where he can score on a wild pitch, error, ground out, sacrifice fly, or base hit. The biggest variable in this situation is whether you hit right- or left-handed. For my money— and perhaps I'm showing my left-handed prejudice here—it's much easier for a righty to handle this advance. Two reasons: It's easier for a righty to "inside-out" a pitch to the right side; and if a righty wants to bunt the man over, he can use a push bunt to the second or first baseman. (I would guard against trying to drop a bunt down the third-base line. Unless it's perfect, the pitcher or catcher will cover it, either holding the runner at second or throwing him out at third. Only a bunt that forces the third baseman to field the ball far enough in front of the bag to prevent him from reaching back and tagging the runner will work.)

For the left-handed hitter, getting the runner over requires a bit more planning, a finer touch. The pitcher, wary of your pulling a pitch, is more than likely working you away. To pull

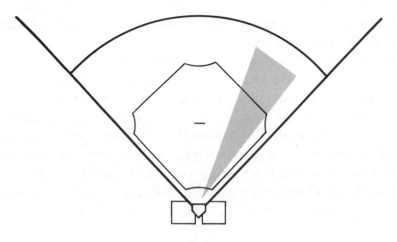

Target zone: moving a runner from first to second

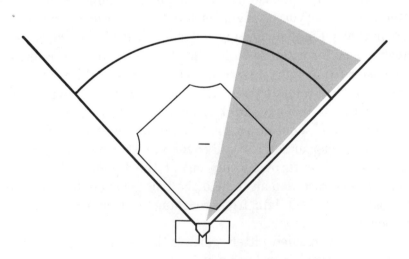

Target zone: moving a runner from second to third

a pitch in the middle of the plate means increasing the influence of the top hand during the swing. I don't mean rolling your wrists, just forcing your top hand through quicker to get the bat head out in front of the plate. Your hands should still be flat on contact, but the barrel end of the bat will be closer to the pitcher.

You should also consider the count. With no strikes, or one strike, if the pitch is not one you can pull, take it, even if it's a strike. Or, better yet, you might try this trick: Move closer to home plate, crowding the inside corner. Maybe the catcher will notice this and, for the sake of a quick out, signal for a heater inside. His thinking might be that the pitcher can jam you, get the weak pop-up or ground ball. But since you set this scam up, you know what he's thinking; you're prepared for the hard stuff inside. So you release your hands a little earlier. You think bat speed and bat head. And you pull that pitch on the ground to second, easily advancing the runner. With two strikes, a good pitcher has greater leverage, much more control over the situation, so you can't be worried about a shifting defense or hitting a ball into a specific area (unless, of course, a manager insists you try, despite the count). Instead, you should concentrate on contact and putting the ball in play. Don't overswing. As time and your baseball skills improve, you can begin to think contact and advancement. Juan Beniquez of the Baltimore Orioles is a master at advancing the runner with two strikes. He's got remarkable bat control.

Situation 2: Runner Stealing Second

Let me give you an example of how we handle this situation with the Angels. Gary Pettis has tremendous speed and is an accomplished base stealer. Nine times out of ten, when Gary's on base, he's thinking, "I'm going." In that case, if there are no outs or one out, and I'm batting behind Gary, I take a strike. I'm willing to reduce my strike allotment by one third so that Gary gets a chance to move into scoring position. If he doesn't go and you take a strike, then you simply resume normal hitting. You should not consider taking a strike as a disadvantage. As you help the runner, he is helping you. You benefit because he's causing the pitcher to split his attention and not concentrate fully on getting you out. He's also helping you because you'll see more fastballs from a pitcher trying to reduce the runner's chances of stealing second. But if you let him steal and he's successful, now you've opened the game up and changed the situation. Now the situation looks like this: Less than two outs, and a runner on second. Now you can move the man over with a bunt or ground ball to the opposite side, setting up a sacrifice-fly situation. See how the simple matter of taking one strike in the right spot can, in the end, mean the difference between scoring and not scoring?

Okay, in this situation, when it's necessary, what's the easiest way to tell the runner you're taking a pitch? There's really a couple of ways. You can talk about the situation before the game or the at-bat, letting him know you're taking a strike every time he's on base with less than two outs. You can also set up some silent code between you, a tip of the cap, a tap of the bat on your right shoe, anything simple—and visible—that tells your teammate you're taking. That way you'll avoid embarrassing and frustrating situations such as this: 2-0 count, runner stealing without your knowledge, and you rip a line drive that is easily turned into a double play.

Important: If the runner isn't as quick—say a Gary Carter instead of a Gary Pettis—I'd give away a strike only if so instructed by the third-base coach or manager.

Sometimes, in the case of a slower runner who is ordered to steal, you can help him out. The best way to help out is to block the catcher's view, to disrupt the catcher's timing. Or just drop your bat into the strike zone (don't keep it there too long or the umpire may call a swinging strike). Pull it out as the pitch approaches. Also, you could bend over the plate a bit—nothing drastic, just enough to disrupt the catcher's timing and release. That extra millisecond or two it takes for the

catcher to move around you might make the difference between a safe or out call at second.

Situation 3: Hit-and-Run

Runner on first, less than two outs. Runner stealing. You're
expected to protect him, ideally getting a base hit into the area
vacated by the infielder who covers second base. The cardinal
rule here is: *Hit the ball anywhere on the ground.* You don't
want fly balls. You don't want line drives. Your job is to hit a
ground ball. Where you hit this ball obviously depends on the
pitch. Normally, the shortstop will cover for left-handed hitters, the second baseman for right-handers. For me, it's a bit
different, thanks to my reputation as an opposite-field hitter
(the shortstop normally stays put, eliminating my favorite hole).
But no matter who covers, don't try to adjust *during* the pitch.
If the second baseman is covering and it's a fastball outside,
don't try at the last second to hit the ball into the hole at second. It won't work. If the ball is away, get it in play some-
place, anyplace. You have to put it in play. Just think "Hit the
ball on the ground."

Do you have to swing at every pitch when the hit-and-run is
called? You do if your manager says so. But sometimes, if there's
a good speed at first and the pitch is in the dirt, you might
want to hold up, not wasting a swinging strike. Of course, with
Larry Leadfoot on the move, you've got to protect him no matter where the ball is pitched, even if you foul the ball off. Finally, don't try to overpower the pitch. Think contact and try
not to uppercut.

When to Use the Hit-and-Run

Here a bit of baseball strategy mixed in with the situations. Of
course, whether your team plays the speed game or relies on
the long ball depends on your players. The Boston Red Sox,
with their long-ball lineup, had little use for the hit-and-run in
1985. The strategy for a team built for the quaint confines of

Fenway Park was power over speed. Playing the power game in Fenway generates more runs than it would, say, on the Astroturf of Busch Stadium in St. Louis. In Fenway, you don't want to give up outs at second base when you have four or five potential twenty-home-run hitters in the lineup. On other teams, however, like Kansas City and St. Louis, the "rabbits" set the table for guys like Brett, Steve Balboni, and Jack Clark. You let guys like Willie Wilson and Vince Coleman run because you've got excellent contact hitters like Willie McGee and Tommy Herr in St. Louis and, in Kansas City, Brett and Hal MacRae hitting behind them. Most of us can handle the bat well enough to take a strike, let the man steal, then move him over to third with a ground ball. But if you've got a slow runner on first, I say forget the steal and go with the hit-and-run. It's a play that I love yet see less and less of each year.

Situation 4:
Lefty vs. Lefty and Righty vs. Righty

One of the things that bothers me most these days is the notion that lefties can't hit lefties and righties can't hit righties. Managers have taken an advantage (or possible advantage) situation and applied a universal application. Yes, a left-handed pitcher has a slight advantage over a left-handed hitter because his curveball breaks away. But, I have to tell you, I didn't get 3,000-plus hits batting exclusively against right-handed pitchers. Good hitters hit all pitching. For some reason, with more coaches going to a platoon system, kids are starting to believe they can't hit left-handers if they're left-handed themselves. Don't believe it. A righty with a .300 average has a better chance of getting a hit off a right-handed pitcher than a lefty with a .250 average.

What happens when you face a pitcher coming from the same side as you is a tendency to bail out, or pull off the ball. Knowing this, you must discipline yourself to stay in there, to keep your head on the ball, to force yourself to be aggressive mentally. Drill it in: Don't give an inch. And if you make an out, it's not because you're both right-handed or both left-handed. It's because pitchers get .300 hitters out 7 out of 10 times.

Situation 5: Relief Pitching

A word to the wise: Don't let it shake you up. So they throw hard. Big deal. If you know who the pitcher is, what's up his sleeve, you can compete. You have some advantages, too. When a reliever comes in, especially to snuff out a threat, his job is to throw strikes. You know the ball is going to be around the plate. And with certain guys—like Goose Gossage in San Diego, Bob James in Chicago, and Dave Righetti of the Yankees—90 percent of the time it's going to be the fastball. Nothing fancy. Just some heavy heat, but if you're geared for it, you're on even terms.

Of course, at the high-school level or below, relief pitching isn't so predictable. Sure, they *want* to throw strikes, but can they? Here you want to be a bit more cautious. Don't expect anything; just work the count as you would with any other pitcher (advantage to you on 2-0 or 3-1; to the pitcher on 0-1 or 0-2). Anticipate hard stuff when he's behind in the count, off-speed stuff when you're in a hole, but don't commit to it ahead of time. It's a good idea in high school to keep a notebook on the pitchers you face, just as many major-leaguers do. That way, come tournament time, or during a league playoff, you can look up ol' Number 27 and see what he was throwing three weeks earlier.

Situation 6: Hitting with the Infield In

The easiest way to hit .500 is when the infield is playing you in. Your goal should be to hit the ball hard on the ground somewhere. Anywhere. Playing in, the infielders have a drastically reduced range. They have little chance of making a play on the ball unless it is hit directly at them. Still, for some unknown reason, hitters feel compelled to try to hit the ball over or through people. Forget it. Hit the ball hard on the ground.

Situation 7: Being a Hero

World Series time. Bottom of the ninth, bases loaded, two outs. Score tied, or one run down. Think fast now. Would you want to be in that situation? I would. You know why? Because anytime I can get a base hit to win a ball game, I want to. I can go back to 1982 and vividly recall the last out of the season for the California Angels. I made it. We were in the American League Championship Series and Brian Downing was at the plate with Ron Jackson on second representing the tying run. I remember telling myself, "C'mon, Brian, give me a shot!" At that moment, I felt I was going to get the base hit to tie the game for us. I got my chance, went to the plate feeling more confident than ever, and I hit a bullet—unfortunately it was right into the glove of Brewer shortstop Robin Yount.

But that's life. I always want to win a game for my club. So should you. Why put it on someone else's shoulders? You're prepared. You've studied the pitcher. This is what the game is all about. If you fail, fine; you did your best. But take a deep breath, step into the box, and accept the challenge.

Situation 8: Pinch-Hitting

There are two kinds of pinch-hitters. One group specializes in pinch-hitting, guys like Rusty Staub in New York. That's their job. That's why they're playing in the big leagues today. The other, much more common group consists of young nonregulars and veterans too old to play every day. No matter what the category, one premise prevails: *You have to realize your role on the club is going to be judged, at least in part, on how you perform in the pinch.* So take it seriously. You must learn to control the mental drudgery, the frustrations, not getting too high or too low. Work to be prepared. How do you do that? By taking extra pregame hitting. By using the hours of extra time you have in the dugout to your best advantage. By concentrating on getting a good swing on every pitch. By knowing what you want to accomplish and how to accomplish it.

In my mind, when you leave the bench to pinch-hit, you're not going up there to take a strike (unless the situation specifically dictates it). You're up there to get on base or win a game. So swing the bat. A lot of well-prepared pinch-hitters will jump on the first good pitch they see, simply because they know they're not going to see too many good pitches if they get behind in the count. Of course, on occasion that strategy will backfire, as it did even to a hitter as good as Hal McRae in a crucial World Series situation against John Tudor of the Cardinals in 1985. McRae, normally the designated hitter for Kansas City, had been relegated to the bench by the rule calling for the DH to be used in the Series only in even-numbered years. McRae was called to pinch-hit in the seventh inning of the fourth game of the Series, bases loaded, his team trailing 3-0. Now, McRae is a notorious first-ball hitter. Tudor knew that. So instead of feeding him a fastball, to get ahead in the count (McRae probably would have taken a terrific cut at it), Tudor nibbled on the outside corner with a sinker. The overanxious McRae took the bait, tapping a harmless ground ball to third. So much for the threat.

The moral here, obviously, is not to fall into a pattern as a pinch-hitter. Sure, be ready for the heater; you're going to see it 80 percent of the time in this situation, particularly in close games with runners on base. But, by the same token, have confidence in your ability to hit with two strikes. Build that confidence by working on just that situation during batting practice. Pretend the count is 1-2, 2-2, or 3-2. You have to swing on the next pitch. Do that over and over each day, hundreds of times. When you finally get into that situation during a game, you'll have the confidence to know you can deliver.

It's also important to stay "in the game," even when you're on the bench. Don't look into the stands or spend time making

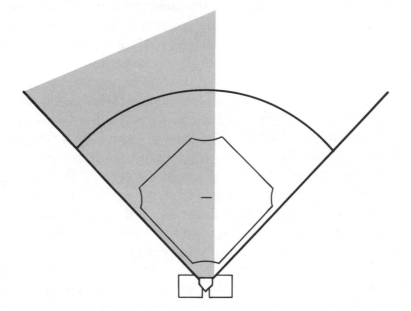

This is my primary target area when hitting away: up the middle/ opposite field

idle chatter. Of course, it helps if the manager tells you an inning or two beforehand to get ready, but, honestly, some managers are too busy. So it's up to you. You have to follow the game from the first out, thinking ahead to situations. Who's been pitching middle relief for this team? What pitches do they use when they're ahead? These are all questions one asks before a game anyway, but they become doubly important in a pinch-hitting situation. You have only one shot at hitting—not three or four—so prepare yourself to make the best of it.

Pinch-hitting isn't just a mental game. You should stretch out vigorously before a game, then plan to work your arms and legs between innings. When the call comes, you're not going to have five minutes to get loose. You might get sixty seconds for a couple of knee bends and trunk twisters. You have to be ready. That means swinging a weighted bat between innings, in the clubhouse or behind the bench. As you swing, concentrate on fundamentals: head down, quick bat, weight transfer, keeping the front shoulder in.

Also, if you're not starting because of a manager's decision or a personal slump, don't sulk. You never know what might happen. If a teammate gets hurt or ejected, you might be in as early as the first inning. If you're not loose or involved in the game, you're nothing but an automatic out. That's one of the things I respected most about my California Angels manager, Gene Mauch. If I wasn't playing, he'd tell me up front, warning me, "If the game get close, or they change pitchers, I want you ready." That's all a ballplayer can ask of his manager. You can't expect them to babysit you.

Situation 9: Designated Hitting

At this point in my career, I may be a lot closer to this role than I sometimes care to admit. Designated hitting has been a thorny issue since its introduction in the American League in 1973. The "purists" object to its use, bemoaning lost strategy. "Reformists" insist it adds runs—and excitement—to the game. Pro or con, it's tough to DH. You're basically being asked to pinch-hit four or five times in a game. The mental strain is rough; you hit and return right to the bench, unable to erase mistakes or frustrations with some fancy fielding. Again, the key here is preparation. Go to the clubhouse or behind the bench and swing a bat, hit a ball off a batting tee, or get someone to soft-toss you pitches you can hit into a net. Do whatever you can to stay loose. Jog easily behind the bench. Stay mentally sharp. One big difference between a good DH and a mediocre one is in their mental approach. You have to steel yourself to the situation, accepting, for the moment, that you're a hitter and nothing more. And if you make an out, accept it. Yes, you should analyze why (bad swing, bad pitch, etc.), but don't dwell on the past—bad or good. You can't labor over any at-bat. If you do, the mental strain will wear you down and you'll end up playing full time again—but it will be in the minor leagues.

Nine

---◆---

BUNTING

"Rod Carew is one of the best bunters the game has
ever seen."

Steve Garvey
1974 National League MVP

Bunting has become a lost art in the game of baseball. Players
today are so caught up in hitting the ball into the seats, even
in batting practice, they forget—or, worse, don't care—enough
to hone their other skills. The result: When the time comes for
them to sacrifice a runner over, or squeeze him home, or beat
out a drag bunt to start a rally, they fail miserably, disgracing
themselves, often contributing to a team defeat. Two of the
best bunters of the past twenty-five years have been great power
hitters, Mickey Mantle and Steve Garvey. Mantle was very
smart, and, before injury took its toll on his legs, a very speedy
player. He knew full well the wisdom of a good bunt. Garvey,
on the other hand, is such a perfectionist it's only natural he
would want to develop *all* his skills. I think he's the premier
two-strike bunter in the National League today.

Both players value the bunt for more than the occasional base
hit or, if the situation calls for it, for the means by which to
move a baserunner over. Those are obvious. Often overlooked
is how the bunt causes the third baseman to cheat in at the

corner, thereby decreasing his range and reaction time to a ball hit in his direction.

I've read recently that I don't bunt for base hits now as much as I did earlier in my career. That's true. In my early days, I'd pick up 20 to 30 hits a year on bunts. One year I was 28 for 34. I don't run as well as I used to, and, perhaps more important, third basemen around the league have gotten wise to me. Now, with them playing in, I pick up 15 to 20 hits a year by slapping the ball past them. So, though I don't bunt for as many hits as I once did, I can directly attribute a similar number of base hits to the threat of a bunt.

The Sacrifice Bunt

The first thing a hitter must understand when he's in a sacrifice situation is he has one job at the plate and one job only—to advance the runner. The term "sacrifice" means just that: "giving up" your at-bat for the good of the team. Forget about bunting for a base hit; get the ball on the ground and advance the runner over. Think "we" instead of "I."

To be successful, remember that bunting is no different from any other form of situational hitting. The basics remain the same. You must look for a pitch that you can handle. In a bunt situation, that means a pitch in the top half of the strike zone. One of the keys to being a good bunter is the angle of your bat upon contact with the ball. You have to keep the barrel end of the bat slightly higher than the handle. If you drop the barrel, the bat head has an overwhelming tendency to angle toward foul territory, and the ball either strikes the top half of the bat (popping up) or is steered foul, neither of which suits your purpose. Since you have to drop the barrel to bunt a low pitch, you're better off looking for one from the waist up.

What about the sacrifice bunt? The conventional way of teaching it is for the hitter to square around—something I've never felt comfortable with. Instead, I favor only a slight pivot of my feet and upper body, which minimizes movement of my

This is the traditional method for teaching the sacrifice bunt. Take your normal stance. Square your body off so it is facing the shortstop (second baseman if you're right-handed), and slide your top hand 3 to 3½ inches up the bat. Keep your eye on the ball, the bat head higher than the handle, and let the ball come to the bat. Try it. If you like this method and if it feels comfortable to you, stay with it.

head and body. This bunting alignment is also more comfortable, as my position in the batter's box is similar to my normal hitting stance. More important, I can see the ball better. As a hitter, you are accustomed to seeing the pitch in a certain way. If you're a lefty, your right eye is closer to the pitcher; the opposite if you're right-handed. When a batter squares all the way around and both eyes face the pitcher, he sees the pitch from a different perspective as it approaches the plate. With my pivot system, your head is in the same position for the bunt as when you hit normally; therefore, you're going to see the ball approach the plate in the same way you see every other pitch. That's obviously to your advantage.

Now, let's get a little more technical. When I walk into the batter's box to sacrifice bunt, nothing changes from my regular stance: I set up in the exact same position in the batter's box; I grip my bat with the same loose and comfortable grip; I prepare to hit as if I'm going to take a full swing. Now, as the pitcher comes set, I make my move, pivoting on my toes, my heels moving clockwise about three inches. This forces my lower body around so that my belt buckle is now facing toward the shortstop (second baseman if you're right-handed). My head and upper body have not moved. My knees are bent slightly and my weight is on the balls of my feet.

As you make the pivot, the top hand slides up the bat about 3 to 3½ inches. The bottom hand becomes the anchor of the bat, the top hand the rudder. At this point, I like to take the index finger of my top hand and point it down the back of the bat. This, combined with the shortened bat, provides great bat control, ensuring a soft grip—another key to good bunting. You want those hands to be soft on the bunt. You don't want to "choke" your bat with a death grip, because a tight grip will cause the ball to jump off your bat upon contact. A soft grip deadens it.

Now, I've made my pivot and have my hands in position on the bat. Step three occurs as the ball is in flight. I make a circular motion clockwise with the barrel end of the bat. Re-

I suggest pointing your index finger down the shaft of the bat when you grip it on the bunt. It will keep your hands soft on the bat, and give you better bat control.

member we talked about how important it is to keep the barrel of the bat higher than the handle? In watching hitters, I've noticed that when they square around, they immediately put their bats into the bunting position. What happens is that as they watch the pitch, the fat end of the bat has a tendency to drop during the anticipatory period, causing foul balls. The little circular motion of the bat I've developed is a discipline that allows me to keep the barrel end of the bat up. It's been a major factor in my success as a bunter.

As you can see, there's a lot going on, and we've yet to make contact. The last step prior to contact is to move the bat from 12 o'clock into the 2-o'clock position. The key to making good contact as a bunter is the exact opposite of what we teach for making good contact as a hitter. In hitting, the action we initiate thrusts the head of the bat toward the ball. In bunting, we want to let the ball come toward the bat. A big mistake bad

One of the most important fundamentals of being a good bunter is keeping the barrel of the bat higher than the handle. When the barrel end drops below the handle end, the drastic angle of the bat will almost always cause the ball to go foul. These two pictures clearly illustrate the difference between right and wrong.

bunters make is trying to jab the bat toward the ball. Once you've moved your bat into the bunting zone, the only time that bat, or any part of your body, should move is when the ball actually makes contact with the bat. I like to call it catching the ball with your bat. That's really what bunting is.

Okay, let's try it. Place your bat into the anticipated line of flight of the ball. Your hands should hold the bat softly, so softly that at impact the bat gives slightly as the ball drops to the ground. Picture the bat "catching" the ball, being the fielder, not the hitter.

All right, let's review some keys to successful sacrifice bunting:

1. Go up to the plate intent on making an "out" to help your team.
2. Look for a pitch in the upper half of the strike zone to bunt.
3. Pivot your lower body while keeping your head and upper body still.
4. Keep the barrel end of the bat higher than the handle end.
5. Grip the bat as loosely as possible.
6. Let the ball come to the bat.

With all that in mind, I must confess it's the way I *teach* the sacrifice bunt. It's not exactly the way I *do* it. There is only one difference in what I teach and what I do, and it's a worthwhile pointer for advanced bunters. I no longer slide my hands up the handle of the bat prior to bunting. The reason I like "novice" bunters (this can include big-leaguers) to slide their hands up the bat is that it gives them less bat to control. As a good bunter, I've advanced to the point now where the bat feels like an extension of my hand. I like to have more bat to work with, so I do everything I teach, except that I keep my hands together at the end of the bat. Either way is correct. But it's best to master the novice method before attempting a technique requiring a more delicate touch.

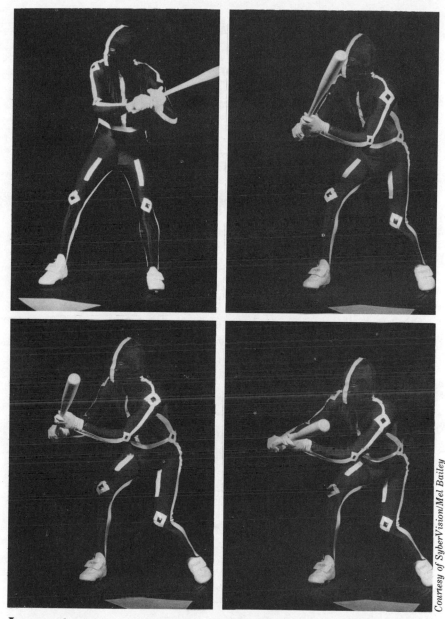

Courtesy of SyberVision/Mel Bailey

I use, and teach, a pivot system for the sacrifice bunt. I believe it's more effective, and more comfortable for me because the stance is so similar to my normal batting stance. Compare the diamonds on my body suit and see how little movement there is in this bunting motion.

The white bat in these photos also shows that small, circular, clockwise motion I use to help me keep the barrel end of the bat higher than the handle end while I am awaiting the ball.

Bunting for a Base Hit

First of all, let's dismiss the myth that it's harder for a right-handed hitter to bunt for a base hit than it is for a left-handed hitter. Granted, a left-handed hitter is one step closer to first base, but three of the all-time best bunters—Phil Rizzuto, Mantle, and Garvey—achieved great success bunting from the right side.

In bunting for a base hit, I prefer the "crossover" method, so called because as the pitch approaches, my back leg steps, or crosses, over the front leg as it moves toward the pitcher, to become, in effect, my first step toward first base. But note that I said my crossover step is *toward the pitcher*. That way, I'll be in optimum position to bunt an outside pitch down the third-base line or an inside pitch down the first-base line. If I make the mistake of having my crossover step take me toward first base, my balance is affected and I'm unable to bunt the outside strike. My momentum is taking me in the opposite direction.

There are two other big differences between bunting for a base hit and for the sacrifice. One is the element of surprise. More bunted base hits can be attributed to the surprise factor than to great execution. Here, right-handed hitters have an advantage over left-handed hitters, if only because infielders don't normally expect right-handed hitters to bunt. They play deeper at the corners. Sure, they'll shorten up when a Willie Wilson or an Alan Wiggins is batting right-handed, but generally, fielders cheat more for lefties.

You can work the surprise factor to your advantage, and I'll show you how. Needless to say, the "foul ball on a third strike and you're out" rule intimidates most players and coaches. But not Mantle, not Garvey. And even with my reputation as a bunter, I went 12 for 12 one year on two-strike bunts. Many of those hits turned into runs that helped us win ballgames. And think what a difference 12 for 12 made to my batting average.

On a sacrifice bunt, forget the surprise element. Everyone

This is the crossover method used in bunting for a base hit. Surprise is a key to bunting for a base hit, so try to delay your crossover move for as long as possible. Notice how when I make my crossover step, it is *toward the pitcher*. My weight stays on the left foot after the crossover . . . my head is on the ball . . . the barrel of the bat is higher than the handle . . . and the ball is headed toward the target area down the third-base line.

in the ballpark knows you're going to bunt, so just take your time, get set, then execute, placing the ball on the ground in a position where anyone but the catcher has to make the play. This is difficult, though, when you're bunting for a base hit. Then you want to delay your mechanics as long as possible, not making your initial move until just before the pitcher releases the ball. This allows plenty of time to take a crossover step, pick up the spin and location of the ball, and get your bat into bunting position. Conversely, there's not enough time for an infielder who's playing back to field a well-placed bunt and throw you out.

Okay, delaying the crossover step and the element of surprise are two keys to a successful "drag bunt." Another is the distribution of your weight and your takeoff to first base. On the sacrifice, no matter whether you're right- or left-handed, your weight will be fairly evenly distributed on the balls of your feet. Not so in base-hit bunting. If you're left-handed and crossing over (as you should be), all your weight should be on the left foot at the moment of contact. That foot, in effect, becomes your starting block toward first base.

For a right-handed hitter, all of his weight will naturally be on his left foot as he steps forward upon contact. Whereas a lefty will cross over and drop his bat into bunting position, a right-handed bunter should shift his body weight and momentum forward, as if he's starting to run, as his bat drops down into the bunting zone. The weight on the left foot again becomes the starting block for the race toward first base. Remember, a key to bunting for a hit is no wasted motion. So drop the bat at contact. Forget about it; just open your hands and let it fall. Your energies should be concentrated on getting down the line; let someone else worry about the bat. If you're lucky, maybe the catcher will trip over it.

So, as you can tell, there are two basic differences in bunting for a base hit: (1) You delay your bunting mechanics in order to take advantage of the element of surprise, and (2) your weight is on your left foot rather than evenly distributed. Everything

When you bunt for a base hit from the right side, your first step (your stride) is toward the pitcher. As you await the ball and move your bat into position, all your weight is transferred to that front foot just prior to contact.

else is the same: You still want to look for a pitch you can handle that's up in the strike zone. If you're left-handed, an outside pitch goes down third; an inside pitch goes down first (and vice versa for right-handers). The barrel of the bat is higher than the handle and motionless upon contact. Keep a soft grip on the bat. And let the ball come to the bat and "catch" it upon contact.

Positioning the Ball on the Bunt

For some players, getting a bunt in fair territory is asking a lot, but as you practice more and more, and begin to build your confidence, you'll get more and more aggressive, more clinical in your attempts. Personally, I drop most of my bunts down the third-base line, especially when I'm bunting for a base hit. You cut it too close when you bunt down the right side. You have to bunt the ball hard enough to get it between the pitcher and the first baseman so that the second baseman has to field it. On the other hand, when you bunt down the third-base line, it's usually a one-man play. The third baseman has to field the ball on the run, often bare-handing it, and make a long throw, usually off balance. Even if the pitcher fields the ball down the line, a righty must stop his momentum, plant, and throw. What's worse (or better, in our case) is when a lefty has to turn his body all the way around before he can make the long throw to first. So you can see why I feel my chances of bunting a base hit down the third-base line are 80 percent higher than if I go down first.

In a sacrifice situation, there is only one crucial rule to keep in mind: Bunt the ball far enough so that the catcher cannot field the ball on the dirt. Preferably, don't let the catcher field the ball at all. Otherwise, on a sacrifice, just place the ball so that you don't bunt it right to a charging infielder. That means keeping your eyes open and head up—seeing who's moving in what direction. Normally, if you can make an infielder alter his charge even one step, it's enough to ensure a successful sacri-

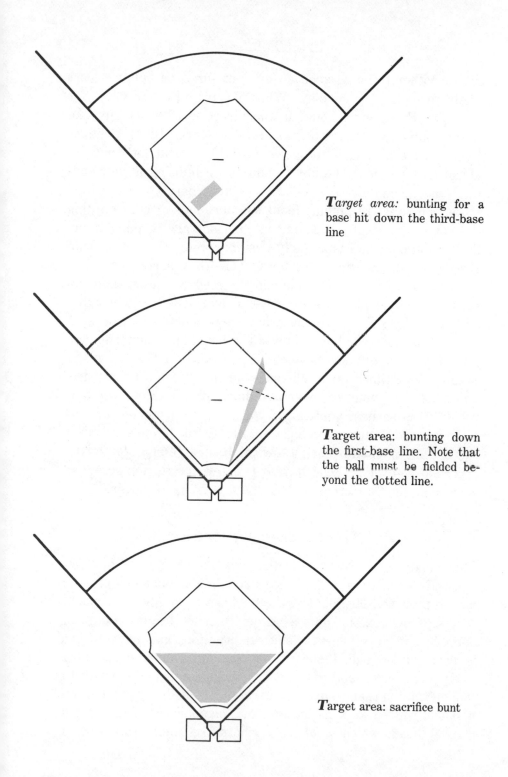

Target area: bunting for a base hit down the third-base line

Target area: bunting down the first-base line. Note that the ball must be fielded beyond the dotted line.

Target area: sacrifice bunt

fice. Another thing to keep an eye out for is the player least likely to make a good play. When we play Kansas City, for example, I'm going to bunt in the direction of a big guy like Steve Balboni ten times before I'll give George Brett a chance to throw me out. He's too great an athlete. But let's not get ahead of ourselves. The key to successful bunting is getting a pitch that will allow you to place the ball where you want to.

As long as we're talking about location, let's discuss bunting the curveball, or any breaking pitch. Contrary to popular belief, a breaking ball is actually easier to bunt than a fastball. Breaking balls are much easier to see, they arrive with less velocity, and are usually higher in the strike zone on their approach to home plate. And as we've mentioned, pitches that are up in the strike zone are what we're looking for, because we want to keep the barrel end of the bat higher than the handle. However, you also have to be prepared for the low pitch, because sometimes that's all that's on the menu. In that case, you must bend your knees and go down after it. Keep the barrel head up as best you can; if you have to drop too far, the pitch is more than likely a ball, so take it. But if you must alter the bat alignment to reach a low pitch, just remember to concentrate even more. You have a greater margin for error, so something has to increase—and that's your mind power.

The Suicide Squeeze

The suicide squeeze is one of the most exciting plays in baseball and will *always* result in a score when the batter executes his job properly. His job: Get the bunt down on any given pitch. A suicide squeeze is the only time when we forget several of our disciplines. When in a suicide situation, you have to get your bat on the ball. If the pitch is low and away and you have to drop the barrel end of the bat to make contact, it's better to foul off a pitch than to have your runner picked off. If the pitch is out of the strike zone, go out and get it. Even if the ball is at your head, which is where pitchers are taught to throw in this situation, you still have to find a way to get the bat on the ball.

Practicing Bunting

I began this chapter by calling bunting a lost art. Where it was lost was in the practice cage, just like so many other aspects of hitting. If you want to improve, you have to pay a price. So many good young players with great speed believe all they have to do is drop the ball down and beat it out. It doesn't happen. You have to know how, where, and when to bunt before it's going to seriously affect your average. And there's only one way to accomplish these things: through practice.

If you're just learning to bunt, don't expect miracles. Start off with thirty minutes a day, just getting the feel of the bat hitting the ball at a speed you can comfortably handle, slowly reviewing, step by step, the mechanics of the sacrifice bunt. After a while—maybe several weeks—the mechanics will become second nature to you. Gradually, as your confidence increases, so should the velocity, speed, and variety of pitches you practice bunting. Don't fret if you feel you're taking a step backward (your proficiency may drop off initially), because soon you'll be able to handle the hard stuff as well as breaking pitches. Now, once you've completed that course, go all the way back to the beginning and start over with bunting for a base hit. Thirty minutes a session, moderate speed. Practice the mechanics. Then, as you gain proficiency, speed up the pitches and start to practice bunting breaking balls.

Once you're sure you've got control over the mechanics, begin bunting into target areas. Place two or three baseballs in various spots down the third-base line, then practice bunting toward those target balls in sequence. After you've practiced hitting targets down the third-base line, go through the same drill down the first-base line. This is the same system I use to stay sharp in the off-season. (Bunting, like hitting, isn't an art you can take out of the closet anytime you want and expect to

Always practice with a purpose. Here I use baseballs as a target for where I want my bunts to stop. (I'd like to take those 11 with me for next season.)

be effective. It takes work all year round.) Pregame batting practice is also a time to take your bunting seriously. Most players rush through their bunts so they can rip easy lobs over the fence. Resist that temptation. Take your time. Have a purpose; ask the BP pitcher to throw you several outside pitches while you practice bunting those balls down the appropriate line. Then have him throw you several inside pitches to bunt. Remember, bunting time during pregame batting practice is limited, so use it wisely. Don't spend too much time bunting; three or four sacrifice and drag bunts down each line is plenty, provided you're concentrating. You can always go out early or stay late, or every so often, on a practice day, take some extra bunting practice. It's the only way I know to master the art.

Ten

◆

BATTING PRACTICE AND CONDITIONING

"Rod Carew is one of baseball's greatest hitters because he works at it year round."

Billy Martin

Hitting is a subtle science, one I feel you can never learn enough about, and one in which I quickly profess to have no omnipotent powers. More often than not these days, I react rather than think, my body and mind fused by the years I've spent whacking ball after ball in practice.

In all those years, three important lessons have been learned. They are *concentration*, *purpose*, and *working on a weakness*. Because practice is the only place suggestions and instruction can be experimented with, it's imperative you develop sound work habits. Hitting .300 is a goal; it means devoting time, energy, and concentration. That's one of the biggest changes in the game today: So many of the kids coming up just don't focus on the job at hand. They see practice as a social hour, a chance to show their strength, or simply to fool around. They think once they've "made it" in the big leagues, work automatically stops. It doesn't. In fact, the smart players work even harder, picking up tips from experienced players and managers. They use the facilities and the coaching to improve their skills.

And that's where *purpose* comes in. You must come to practice every day with a definite goal in mind. (You want to work on hitting curveballs. You need help on the drag bunt. In the field, you need to get rid of the ball quicker on the double play. Anything.) You don't have to spend hours on your weaknesses, just as long as you recognize them as weaknesses (believe me, some scout will!) and are devoted to turning a negative into a positive. And don't blame your manager or coach for your miscues or failings. A manager doesn't bunt or move a runner over. You do. To avoid even having to *think* about making such excuses, takes the importance of practice to heart. Learn that *striving* to be a great player will carry into other facets of your life—in school, in business. Planting the seeds of success at an early age can mean a big harvest later on.

As a professional, one who cares greatly about his image and batting average, I work almost year round. I wouldn't even take the four weeks off from hitting that I do in late October except that in order to get the most out of batting practice, I must be physically well enough to continually execute a proper swing. After 30 or so preseason games, 162 regular-season games, and playoffs (if I'm lucky), the body needs a rest.

Preparing for a Season

During the off-season, I try to hit three days a week, usually Monday, Wednesday, and Friday. After four weeks without a bat in my hands, I go back to the basics. I try to make contact, pure and simple, performing a specific action over and over, ten minutes a day, against easy pitching. No matter when you're taking batting practice, it's important to maintain your hitting discipline, to have a purpose for every swing. When I start hitting after a prolonged layoff, I want nothing but straight pitches—"easy heat" I can hit back up the middle.

After three or four weeks of this routine, I'll start asking for breaking pitches, increasing my hitting time from ten minutes to fifteen minutes—never longer. Even during the season, when

A good way to warm up, or to practice your mechanics, is by playing soft toss into a net. Alternating with a partner, have him softly toss you the ball, underhand, as we are doing in the picture. Keep your head on the ball, and practice making good contact.

I'm in peak condition, I won't hit for longer than fifteen minutes. I do this for two reasons. One is that after fifteen minutes, I find my lower back begins to get sore. If I alter my swing to compensate for the soreness, I begin to do unnatural things and pick up bad habits. It's the same when you feel tired. Second, it's difficult to maintain peak concentration and discipline beyond fifteen minutes. You don't want to practice sloppy habits. I've found over the years that if you can get in ten to fifteen minutes of good, solid, disciplined hitting, you've accomplished all there is to do. Why go further? Use the time to work on other parts of your game. Run, ride an exercise bike, take ground balls. It's not a lot to ask during the off-season. Also, consider videotaping yourself to compare periods when you're a hot hitter and when you're slumping. Most important, however, is to try to get the most out of every swing. Do these things and you'll be ready to start helping your team win ballgames from opening day.

In-Season Practice Days

Once the season starts, you have to adapt your batting-practice schedule to your game schedule. If you're a high-school or Little League player, you're playing only one or two days a week, so that leaves you three to five practice days. If you're in college or pro ball, you're playing and/or traveling much more, so your challenge is to *make* the time that is necessary for quality batting practice. Quality BP is different from pregame batting practice, which we will address later.

As discussed, never hit longer than fifteen minutes on any given day, unless you're a switch-hitter. Then hit ten minutes from each side. The first few minutes, just try to get loose and make contact. You want straight pitches right down the middle. Concentrate on your mechanics; think contact. As soon as I'm loose, I start asking the pitcher to spot the ball. Several inside, several outside, a few high and a few low. With these pitches, I work on using my hands, being quick, aggressive, hitting the ball where it's pitched—using the whole field. I do this until I feel satisfied that I've achieved an acceptable level of consistency with my mechanics.

Once I've reached that level, I have my batting-practice pitcher mix up his pitches and their location so I never know whether I'll be seeing a breaking ball or a straight pitch. This forces me to concentrate even more on reading the pitch, reacting to the ball, honing my hitting instincts and mechanics. By this time, my hands are sore, I'm tired, so I conclude my hitting for the day.

I will, however, still bunt. We talked at length about practicing bunting in the previous chapter. But I practice my bunting on practice days the same way I practice hitting. Each pitch demands the utmost in discipline, the utmost in concentration. Each pitch has a purpose. The same discipline I use in a game I use in bunting. Every at-bat is the most important at-bat of my career. And the same goes for batting practice. Every pitch is approached with single-minded concentration.

While we are talking about batting practice, I'd like once again to mention bats. One of the keys to being a good hitter is knowing yourself as a hitter. Some players at lower levels can be deceived by the use of aluminum bats. Aluminum bats give hitters a false sense of their hitting capabilities. I can't tell you how many young players come to work out with us directly from high school or right out of college who can't understand why they don't hit the ball as far as they did "back home." The reason is the aluminum bat. I strongly oppose using them.

Now, I'm not going to be naive enough to believe that, come game time, you're going to put aside your aluminum bat because I say it's deceiving. But I am going to ask you to put it aside in the off-season and on practice days. Take your practice on these days with a wood bat. Learn who you really are as a hitter and what your capabilities are. Then, when you hit with your aluminum bat on game day, you'll be even further ahead.

Aluminum bats are the worst things to happen to hitters since the slider. If you must hit with an aluminum bat in a game, at least do all your practicing with a wood bat so you can get a true idea of your ability.

Game Days

Batting practice on game days serves several important purposes. You want to use it to get loose, to practice proper swing mechanics and lock them into your memory bank, as well as to prepare mentally for the game and for the pitcher(s) you'll be facing that day. Too many players don't treat pregame batting practice with the proper respect. Pregame is the beginning of our day's work. That's something that has caused me difficulty with the press in the past. Once I start work, I don't want to be distracted from the task at hand. I've always been willing to spend as much time as necessary with the press before my workday begins. Once batting practice starts, though, I'm intent on preparing for the game. I have to be, because good hitting demands that kind of attention. It is an attitude that probably won't win too many friends in the media, but it will add points to your average.

On game days, be aware of your opponent's pitchers and what they throw. That's not always the easiest thing to do, but few pitchers make their debut against you. If you're going to see a curveball pitcher, ask for more breaking pitches that day. If he's a fastball pitcher, have a little more zip put on the ball. Also, in pregame batting practice, be aware of what you need to work on. If pitchers have been jamming you lately, have your pitcher throw inside and work on moving your hands through the ball and making good contact.

Pregame batting practice is a time for work, not for horsing around. I can't tell you how often a good session of pregame batting practice translates into a multiple-hit game. Take that from a major-leaguer who has nearly 1,000 multiple-hit games to his credit.

Two other points about pregame batting practice. Whenever possible, try to take a round or two against a right-hander *and* against a left-hander, because even though a righty may start, that doesn't mean you won't see a lefty that day. Prepare yourself for every game. And practice your bunting. You never know when you'll be called on for a suicide squeeze, or to sacrifice a runner to second in hopes of breaking a tight game.

Switch-Hitting

Even in batting practice I've always been fascinated by switch-hitters, how they can hit line drives from one side, then turn around and hit the same shots from the other side. I can't emphasize enough to young kids and parents the edge a switch-hitter has in a game. I would recommend it to any young hitter. Not only does it increase your chances of playing, but, more important, if you're struggling from one side of the plate, chances are the next day you'll be able to turn around and try it from the other side.

How early should a player consider switch-hitting? My estimate is around eight years old, though you could certainly start a bit earlier, working off a tee. But by eight, the player's been given a chance to develop the basic skills. The best ways to teach switch-hitting are with a batting tee or by softly tossing a ball to the player from each side. I'd start out with twenty pitches a day from each side if the player is young, gradually working up to ten or fifteen minutes a day. One thing I've always found intriguing about switch-hitting is how someone can hit .290 from, say, the right side and just .230 from the left. Obviously, this begs the question, Why not hit right all the time? The answers are fairly obvious: One, chances are you'll be platooned against right-handers, and, two, you won't see the same pitches batting solely right-handed as you would switch-hitting.

So what do most hitters do who hit 60 points less from one side than the other? Sadly, not too much. Typically, when you see them working out in the batting cage, they're hitting from their best side, saving the last 20 percent for the "off side." That won't work. It's just like anything else in baseball: If you can't handle hot shots in the hole at short, you get a coach or friend to hit you a hundred ground balls a day to your right

Kevin Reece

Eddie Murray is a perfect example of a switch-hitter who alters his stance from each side of the plate. Notice Eddie batting right-handed. He is very erect, his weight is back, and his front toe is open. From the left side, Eddie has closed down his lead leg and hits from a coiled position.

If you're a switch-hitter, be like Eddie Murray. Treat each side of the plate differently. What's comfortable from one side of the plate may not work from the other. Find out what does work, and go with it.

until you can. If you can't handle the slider or fastball from your weak side, you work on it until you can. You've got to organize your life to allow for more practice from that side. If that means getting to practice an hour early, so be it.

Each day, when practicing switch-hitting, you should aim to alternate from each side. Never take all your swings from one side in anticipation of facing a right-hander or a left-hander. All it takes is one signal to the bullpen from the manager to alter those plans. Also, take BP as a lefty off a lefty. This helps you prepare for pitches that move into your body—screwballs and some cut fastballs—and pitches in the same location with similar spin that you would get from a right-hander.

Should you swing the same from both sides? Definitely not. These are two separate swings, two separate hitters, and should be treated as such. The switch-hitter who displays power from both sides is rare. Mickey Mantle was an exception. So was former Yankee Tom Tresh. And today a guy like Eddie Murray of Baltimore, who has two diametrically opposed stances, can take you deep from either side. But most of you considering switch-hitting or who are switch-hitting right now must come to grips with the kind of hitter you are from each side. Power from the right? Fine. Take a little longer stride; try to uppercut certain pitches. More a line-drive hitter from the left? Great. Work on hitting the ball back up the middle, using your hands, cutting down on the swing.

Whatever the package, it's important not to forget fundamentals: the weight shift, the hands, the rhythm of the stride and swing. In some ways, switch-hitting may double the workload and frustration, but when that work pays off—and it will— it could make the difference between sitting and starting, and eventually, in some cases, the minors or the major leagues.

Conditioning

Because hitting so combines the physical and the mental, the ability of your body to recognize and react to game situations makes a big difference in your performance. This has become more obvious in recent years, with the advent of large salaries in pro baseball. In the old days, conditioning began on the first day of spring training and ended on the last day of the season; today it's a year-round job. The result is that players are playing longer, at higher levels of achievement. You only have to look at some recent statistics to prove that point.

At thirty-seven in 1985, Carlton Fisk was one of baseball's top home-run hitters. At forty-four, Pete Rose broke Ty Cobb's all-time hit record and was still hitting around .270. I hit .339 the year I turned thirty-eight. Why? Conditioning, and overcoming the popular notion that just because you're pushing forty you can't play anymore. Most of you reading this book really won't have to worry about the age factor for quite a while, but you can just as easily get out of shape, and that will affect your abilities as a hitter.

The first thing I'm going to ask you is to stay away from drugs, cigarettes, and alcohol. I'm very concerned about the drug and alcohol problem, not only in the major leagues but in our colleges and schools as well. I've watched players with All-Star talents have their skills drastically reduced by alcohol and drugs. It really doesn't make any difference whether you're a great player or a great fan; those substances can ravage your body and ruin your life. Do yourself a favor: Stay off drugs and booze.

I'm no fan of cigarettes, either. Aside from the long-term possibilities of lung cancer, the immediate effects of shortness of breath and reduced circulation are very detrimental to a player in a game built on speed. Hitting and fielding a baseball is hard enough; you need every physical advantage you can muster. So don't give up that edge; instead, work to excel through conditioning and proper nutrition.

Another problem for ballplayers is curfew. After college, most clubs don't have one. I realize that with scheduling nowadays, with many games played at night and ending near 10 P.M., it's tough to go right home and rest. You want to party. But be careful. What you do at night affects how you play the next day. If you're tired, hung over, worried about a girl, it's going to keep you from concentrating on the job at hand.

When I was in the minor leagues, I didn't have much of a life off the field. First, I was intent on playing the game. Second, I've never liked to drink much. So I played Ping-Pong, went to dinner, relaxed. I'd suggest the same for you. The minor leagues are full of players with the talent to play in the big leagues but, unfortunately, not the discipline. It's tough to say no sometimes, but it's a sacrifice you have to make if you want to be a better player.

There are many things you can do to keep your weight down and stay in shape. For the most part, a comfortable mixture of light weights, stretching exercises, running, and good nutrition will do it. Since you're not training for a triathlon, you really don't need much more than thirty minutes of exercise a day. During the off-season, especially, find an activity or sequence of activities you enjoy, and go to it! Here are some of my favorites:

Walking. I'm really not a big fan of jogging or distance running. In the past, I ran for exercise quite a bit, but I stopped because the constant pounding was taking a toll on my knees and lower back. Three or four days a week, during the off-season, and sometimes during the season, I'll go off on a very brisk fifteen- or twenty-minute walk along a nice, safe route near my home in Southern California. I think you'll find you get as much exercise from a brisk walk as you do from a long, slow jog, with less wear and tear on your body. I do this for half of the week. The other half, I do the following:

Wind Sprints. Not my favorite exercise, but important for building wind and lower-body strength. When you start alternate-day wind sprints, don't make it any more unpleasant than necessary. Start easy. Go out to a nearby track or the outfield of your baseball field and mark off 50 yards. That's long enough. Start off by doing 5 to 7 easy wind sprints. Sprint one way and walk the return route, taking deep breaths in and out. Minimize the stress on your legs by wearing a good, comfortable training shoe rather than your cleats. After several days, start building up to 10, then 15 sprints by adding one a day on your sprint days. Once you reach 15, there is no reason to add more. Work on your speed and improve your ability to maintain good speed throughout all 15 sprints.

Basketball and Racquet Sports. Because everyone doesn't live in a year-round warm climate like I do, it's important to find activities you can do indoors. Basketball, racquetball, and tennis are three of my favorites because they involve constant motion, are good for your wind, demand split-second reactions and decisions, and increase your hand-eye coordination and foot speed, all of which help keep your mind and body sharp for hitting.

Weights. One look will tell you I'm not going to win any Mr. Universe contests, but I do believe in weight training. If you are going to work with weights, stick to flexibility exercises, developing the parts of the body important to your hitting—arms, wrists, forearms. Do 3 sets of 10 to 15 repetitions. And don't increase the weight until you can do all 3 sets. You don't want to bulk up, but you want to be strong.

Hand Exercises. Someone who preaches "hand hitting" as much as I do is going to suggest you have to keep your hands strong. The old "squeezing a tennis ball" exercise has almost become a cliché, but it really does help to strengthen your hands and wrists. And it's so easy to do. I'll squeeze a tennis ball when I'm walking around the house or just sitting and watching TV. I'm to a point now where half the time I'm not even aware I'm doing it.

When I was playing baseball on an exhibition tour in Japan many years ago, I learned an exercise the Japanese use to help

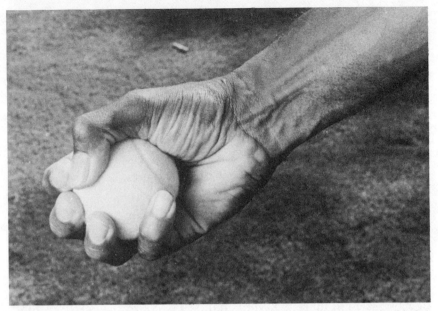

The old, reliable "squeeze a tennis ball" exercise is a good way to build the wrist and forearm strength that's needed to generate good bat speed.

develop hand strength. This exercise utilizes uncooked rice. Take your hands and insert them, one at a time, in a deep bucket of rice. Squeeze the rice and release. Do 5 repetitions of 10 squeezes on a regular basis and you'll feel the difference in your hands, wrists, and forearms.

Another good exercise to help you increase hand strength can be done in your living room. Spread newspaper on the floor and get on all fours. Open your hand as wide as you can and place it in the middle of the spread-out newspaper. Then start squeezing the newspaper, wadding it until you have gathered the entire sheet in your hand.

One additional exercise for your hands is table tennis, which really places a premium on hand-eye coordination. It is important to always try to play with someone better than you. Force yourself to play up to his or her level. You will see your own improvement, and it will help your hitting.

Traditional Exercises. Those exercises that everyone hates and takes for granted in phys. ed. class are great conditioners.

I'm talking about push-ups, chin-ups, and especially sit-ups. You can have the fastest hands in the world, but if you have a soft, unresponsive stomach, you're not going to be able to get your hips into action. So do 50 or 100 sit-ups a day.

Play Ball. One of the best ways to stay in shape for baseball is to play the game. Swing a bat; take ground balls; shag fly balls whenever you can. Don't worry about swinging a weighted bat a hundred times a day. Weighted bats should be used only to help you loosen up. Swing *your* bat. Take batting practice and play ball. That is what's going to help you build bat speed.

Proper Diet

My wife, Marilyn, will laugh every time she looks at this page and sees that I'm writing about proper diet. You see, she knows that I have a sweet tooth and enjoy my share of junk food. But that's okay. I think it's important to mix fun foods into your diet on an occasional basis. Just keep in mind the four basic food groups—dairy, meat and fish, fruits and vegetables, and breads and cereals. You have to build your diet around the above groups, but, to my mind, you don't have to be a fanatic. Enjoy your foods, and if you overdo it one day, cut back a little the next day. I mean, I never met a lemon cake I didn't like. . . .

Though I like to have fun with my diet, I increase my discipline level to its absolute highest on game days. Everybody is different, but if you eat too much *before* a game, you're going to be sluggish *during* the game. I prefer to eat light about four hours before game time, and play the game slightly hungry. This pregame meal can be something as simple as a sandwich or fruit before a night game, or breakfast before a day game. Then, after the game, I'll have my big meal of steak, chicken, or fish, plus vegetables and salad.

During a game, the important thing is to replenish the fluid levels in your body. Stay away from carbonated beverages and

lean toward the Gatorade-type drinks most teams now have—
or, better yet, water. But be careful. Don't drink too much and
get bloated to the point where it's going to hurt you on the
field.

As far as vitamins are concerned, take a multivitamin if you
like, but it's really not necessary. Find a nice combination of
foods from the four basic food groups. Eat well on a daily basis
and you'll get all the vitamins and nutrition you need.

Playing in Pain

My attitude is that if you're hurt, the only person who can
make the decision to play or not is you. Sure, broken legs are
broken legs, but with ankle sprains, hamstring or groin pulls,
the decision is yours. Personally, I won't play with an injury
if I honestly feel playing will cause the team more harm than
good. I watched for years as Oliva tried one machine, one cream,
one shot after another to try to get his ravaged legs into shape.
Six, sometimes seven hours a day of work in the training room.
Home remedies. Once he even tried rubbing a can of STP oil
treatment on his knee. But Tony never quit; he *wanted* to play,
and because of his desire, his influence on a young ballplayer
like myself was immense. It helped me realize if there's any
way you can get on that field, go for it; but, on the other hand,
don't be stupid. If you can't play at a respectable level, sit down,
rest a spell, and let your body recover. In the long run, you're
doing both yourself and your teammates a big favor.

Eleven

◆

TEACHING HITTING

To be a good teacher you have to know what you're talking about. I'm afraid too many coaches today are frustrated ex-jocks who think they know the game but really don't. Yet they demand that a young, impressionable hitter conform to their style of hitting. I would insist that if you want to be a good hitting teacher, you must first seek out and learn the fundamentals of good hitting. You don't necessarily have to be able to physically perform what you're teaching, but you must be acutely aware of just what your beliefs are, how they work together to form important concepts, and know how to explain these concepts clearly and concisely.

Therefore, if you are serious about being a good teacher, you must invest the time necessary to increase your knowledge about the game. In every community there are many college coaches, pro coaches, or ex-pro ballplayers who know good hitting. Seek them out. Talk to them. Find out what they have to say about hitting and apply it to your own teaching.

That's just the first step. I'm also a big believer in clinics and seminars. Any youth organization that hires its own coaches should take the responsibility of educating them. The best seminars and clinics are hands-on sessions given by experienced, professional coaches. By "hands-on" I mean "more than talk."

In every community there are college coaches, pro coaches, ex-pros, and active ballplayers, like Doug DeCinces, pictured here. Seek them out; talk to them; attend their clinics; then incorporate their knowledge into your teaching.

I like to see student teachers on the field, learning for themselves what they should be teaching.

Once you've been to the clinics, it's important to put into action what you've learned. You don't go to a clinic to fortify your own theories; you go to refine and expand and sometimes even unlearn them. Keep an open mind.

The importance of observation can't be overlooked. If you are fortunate enough to live in a city with a major- or minor-league team, get out to the park as often as possible. Don't just show up at game time and watch nine innings. Get out early enough to watch batting practice. If there is no professional franchise nearby, travel to the local university or community college. Watch those players; introduce yourself to the coach; talk baseball. You'll be surprised how pleasant these people can be if you hit them at the right time, after a practice, or around the cage during hitting drills on an off day (definitely not thirty minutes before a game).

Coaches should read a variety of hitting books, as well as watch videotapes on hitting. I recently made a tape for a company called SyberVision that I feel is an excellent observational tool. The name SyberVision is derived from the words "cybernetics" and "vision." Cybernetics is the science of guiding a system (in this case, you) toward an ideal goal state (fundamental hitting skills) through the feedback of goal-relevant information (repeated sensory exposure to a highly skilled model; in this case, me). SyberVision is based on the concept of "neuromuscular programming," a sort of mind-over-muscles philosophy. By watching a role model perform picture-perfect skills, your nervous system processes and adjusts the input until the goal state is realized and maintained.

This leads me to an important new area for teaching hitting: video. I believe that the introduction of video technology is *the* most important discovery in teaching hitting since hard work.

Most of the major-league teams now have video operators who tape every at-bat of every game should the players care to view them. Tony Gwynn of the Padres takes it a step further. His wife, Alicia, goes out to the ballpark each night and tapes every one of his at-bats. After the ballgame, Tony goes straight home to view the tape and evaluate his mechanics. It's no accident that Tony is a batting champion.

Another former batting champion, Keith Hernandez of the Mets, was taught to hit by his father, who now tapes all his games off cable television. During the 1985 season, Keith's dad noticed from one of the tapes that Keith had altered his stance so drastically that his father, looking from a center-field camera angle, couldn't read the number on Keith's back during his setup. A long-distance telephone call followed, and Keith almost immediately broke out of the worst slump of his career and moved his batting average up to the .300 mark. He finished at .309 with 91 RBIs. I'm fortunate to have the SyberVision tape.

When you are going to use film or videotape to help you evaluate a hitter, the two best angles to shoot from are directly in front of the hitter and from the side facing the batter. You'll notice the photos in this book have been taken from these positions. And remember to keep the hitter in your frame from head to toe, so you can evaluate each body part in action.

When we're home, I'll sometimes watch myself on tape two or three times a week following ballgames, just to make sure I haven't lapsed into any bad habits.

My point is that, with the tremendous growth of video and the reduction in the cost of equipment, every serious batting instructor should have a video camera and recorder as part of his teaching equipment. If you're a high-school coach, urge your school to purchase one. If you're a Little League coach, there's a good chance that at least one set of parents out of an entire team will own a unit. And if all else fails, cameras can be rented on a day-to-day basis at very reasonable prices. If all of the parents chip in toward the rental, the cost will be nominal.

The nice thing about taping a youngster hitting is that not only will he hear your instruction but he'll be able to grasp what you're telling him more quickly because he can see himself as well. It allows the youngster to sit and watch himself hit, see what he needs to improve on, and learn from what he does well.

The two ideal viewing angles for videotaping a hitter are from in front of him and from the side facing him; that is, from the first-base side if you're taping a right-handed hitter and from the third-base side if you're taping a lefty. By shooting from the side or front of the hitter, you can see more than you can from any other angle. In front is the best, but obviously impractical in a game situation. And make sure you have the hitter in the picture from head to toe so you can observe all the body parts in action.

If you have unlimited access to a video camera, tape both practice and game situations. If access is limited, tape just game at-bats. During a game situation, we can see how the added mental pressures affect the player's concentration at the plate. A player will more typically show the imperfections of his hitting style in a game situation than in batting practice.

Evaluating a Hitter and Adjusting

The first thing you must keep in mind is that each hitter is an individual and must be evaluated as an individual.

Rod Carew couldn't hit exactly like Don Mattingly, who couldn't hit like Tony Gwynn, who couldn't hit like George Brett. We all have found our own elements of style and comfort within the basic fundamentals of good hitting. Each hitter should experiment and find his own comfortable style of hitting. And a good hitting instructor should give the player enough freedom to develop his own style. Billy Martin says that he never really believed in hitting coaches until he worked with Lou Piniella. That's because Lou takes a customized approach to each hitter. Thus, your biggest challenge as a teacher will be understanding that each hitter's style is unique. You have to watch each hitter without preconceived notions. When he's going good, what is he doing and why? When he's going bad, you have to be able to answer the same questions.

As I touched upon earlier, the best place to observe a hitter is from directly in front of him. In front of the hitter, you can see everything: hand movements, head positioning, the stride (is he stepping out too soon?), a loose front shoulder. Facing a hitter head-on also allows you to see if the hitter has fear of the ball. Most youngsters fear being hit by a pitch. They don't want to get hit, so instead of watching the ball and swinging aggressively, they'll have a tendency to bail out a little and not take their best swing. In a case like this, you have to try to assure them that they are going to get hit at times, and that it will hurt. But the hurt will go away.

The most important thing I try to tell youngsters when I go out and do clinics is to learn how to swing the bat, learn how to be aggressive, and learn how to make contact. Don't worry about getting hit with the baseball, and don't think too much when you're at the plate.

If a player continues to cringe or steps into the bucket when the ball approaches the plate, there are several cures. Take him out with a soft, hollow rubber ball and let the ball hit him several times, but not hard. Part of the fear of being hit is overcoming the fear of the ball's approaching impact. This drill allows the hitter to familiarize his mind and body to the sight and feel of the ball hitting him, helping him overcome a major obstacle.

Now, if a player continually steps in the bucket, it is best to take him back to the basics. Start him off on a batting tee. Tell him to concentrate on one thing: keeping his head on the ball. You can even make a mark on the ground in front of him and have him concentrate on striding into the mark and keeping his head on the ball. Once he seems to be adjusting to that, advance to a soft underhand toss from about ten feet away. Again, have your hitter repeat the process of striding into the ball while keeping his head still and on the ball throughout the swing. This will help program the proper mechanics into the player's memory bank, so that come game time all the drills will pay off.

The Batting Tee

We just talked about using the batting tee to help overcome the fundamental problem of stepping into the bucket. Like the video camera and videotapes, the batting tee is essential equipment for the good coach. In many respects, the batting tee is the Rodney Dangerfield of baseball equipment: It doesn't get any respect. But it does from Rod Carew. Kids laugh at the batting tee as being elementary. But that's how you learn, how you teach—by breaking hitting down to its simplest, most fundamental form.

The tee is so good because it allows young hitters to work on their mechanics. You can work on hitting the ball to the opposite field and practice pulling the ball off the tee, and stride we've already talked about. One of the things to keep in mind when you're practicing off a tee is that the ball is stationary. The player should adjust his stance in relation to the tee, not

Here I'm using the batting tee to practice my mechanics on a pitch that's high and on the outside corner, a good pitch to take to the opposite field. Notice how upright I am and how flat my hands are as they move toward the ball. Now compare the two pictures. My head hardly moves, and there is little difference in my lower body after contact. My hands and arms are doing all the work. When you work off the batting tee, concentrate on repeating proper mechanics so that they become ingrained in your memory bank.

vice-versa. You don't want to have your players practice pulling the ball from the same position that they use to practice going to the opposite field. An outside pitch goes the opposite way; the inside pitch is a pitch you pull. Move the tee for an outside strike when your hitter is practicing going the other way and inside for pulling the ball. Remind your players of the fundamentals—hands, weight shift, stride. You can't lose sight of the basics or your mistakes will ultimately be passed along to your players.

Playing Is More Important Than Winning

In my daughter's Bobby Sox softball league, in order to have an official game, you must complete seven innings within a two-hour time limit or the game is replayed. One day, with time running out and my daughter's team in a comfortable lead, it became obvious that the kids would never finish the game in the allotted time. Rather than accept that, her coach sent her and her teammates up to the plate with the instruction to make an out.

I was quite upset. I don't want kids to learn that you have to "win at all costs." And as a hitter, seeing kids swinging at pitches over their heads or in the dirt for the express purpose of making an out made me shudder.

Good coaches teach good hitting and good hitting practices. You teach your players to be hitters by letting them hit. Hear me: *A walk is not as good as a hit in Little League.* If a kid works a walk while aggressively looking for a base hit, that's good hitting. If a kid goes up to the plate with an 0-0 count hoping for a walk, that's bad coaching.

Unfortunately, there are poor coaches at the Little League level, but you don't have to be one, and you don't have to be quiet if you see one in your league. Fortunately, most Little Leagues have instituted a rule that makes it mandatory for each child to play a specified number of innings in each game.

If your league doesn't have that rule, work to get one introduced.

As a coach, you must understand that the best way to encourage a player's participation and growth is to keep it fun. When players stop having fun, they quit, especially at a younger age. Most Little Leaguers probably won't even play high-school baseball, much less college or professional. Let your players get the most from their ability, and help them along the way. Don't favor one eight-year-old over another because he or she may have better skills. Let them all be exposed to competition, but expose them, too, to a spirit of equality, fairness, and teamwork. Many kids are quiet and shy, and the only time they can really enjoy themselves is on the field. Don't take away a young player's dignity so you can win a game.

Praise and Criticism

We've identified three of the major tools necessary to build great hitters: hard work, video cameras, and a batting tee. There is another major tool you should make use of—and that's praise. I think you should constantly praise young hitters, and I don't think you should ever criticize them. A pat on the back is great, no matter how old you are, whether you're a Little Leaguer or a big-leaguer. Nothing makes you want to work harder than recognition for a job well done. You should also give your players a pat on the back when they don't do well. Reassure them. If they made an out, they'll get another at-bat and another after that. Young hitters discourage easily. Good teachers reassure; they don't criticize.

When I was hurt in 1970, I went to quite a few Little League games. I was embarrassed, upset, and angry, not just at the coaches but at the parents. Children should have the opportunity to go out and have fun and compete with other kids. Don't pressure them from the stands with words like "You're not going to watch any television tonight if you strike out or make a bad play." I think that when you're coaching young kids, instead of

Rod Carew

In its purest sense, baseball is a game for kids to play . . . and to have fun playing. Winning and losing are not important at this level. Playing the game and enjoying it are.

berating a youngster when he makes a bad play you should give him a pat on the fanny. Let him know you're on his side. Don't belabor a bad play; teach the kids so they learn, so they want to play harder, and make sure they understand why it's a bad play and what you expect of them. The best time to correct a player's mistake is directly following the at-bat or error. If he pulled his head, tell him while it's fresh in his mind—and in yours. But do it in a way that the player is reassured that he's one step closer to being a good hitter and confident in his ability as a player and a person.

Coping with Overzealous Parents

Possibly one of the most difficult aspects of coaching young players is overzealous parents. Needless to say, each parent puts his or her child's interests above the rest; it's only natural. But unfortunately some parents take it too far. I think it's important from the start that you make the parents understand, as tactfully as possible, that once the teams are selected, the team is your responsibility. Talk to them about participation, the spirit of teamwork, and the importance of praise. Let them know that winning isn't everything to you, that developing these players is. If they can't accept that, maybe their child should play for another team.

Most important, don't ever let a personality conflict with a parent surface publicly, in front of the other players or their parents, whether it be at the ballpark, a community function, or a gathering at your house. Take it upon yourself to be the mature, rational part of the equation.

If you're a young player or the parent of one, it's important for you to look for the above attributes in your coach or your child's coach. If you're not satisfied that your child's coach has his or her best interests at heart, you should discuss it with the coach. If that has no impact, talk it over with your child. If he is unhappy with this coach for justifiable reasons, consider letting your child change teams—or sports—until the problem can be rectified.

Summary

A good teacher is hard to find. I've had only one in my career, and that's Tony Oliva, a three-time American League batting champion. The reason Tony was—and still is—such a great coach is that he understands athletes and has every one of the following attributes:

- Knowledge of hitting
- Awareness that each hitter is an individual, and the capability to familiarize himself with each individual hitter
- Realization that his job is to help each hitter reach his potential
- Confidence, strength in his own knowledge of hitting, and respect for every player's capacity to learn

Finally, my philosophy is that to be successful, you have to be willing to make mistakes, and to learn from those mistakes. Most coaches went through the same problems and made the same mistakes as children growing up, and they can also make mistakes as adults. So you know youngsters are going to make mistakes, and you can be there to correct those mistakes, to praise the children. You're not there to chew them out, to sit them down on the bench because they walked up and struck out in a situation where they should have gotten a base hit. Sometimes you have to raise your voice, but you'll get more out of your players with praise and a firm set of standards than you will with intimidation.

Twelve

---◆---

CAREW ON BOGGS, BRETT, GWYNN, MATTINGLY, AND MURRAY

The five best hitters in baseball today, and probably into the 1990s, are, in alphabetical order, Wade Boggs of Boston, KC's George Brett, Tony Gwynn of the Padres, the Yankees' Don Mattingly, and Eddie Murray of Baltimore. They've already combined to win six batting titles and will win more, believe me. Brett, Mattingly, and Murray combine power with their ability to make contact. And they use the whole field. Their power comes from natural strength, plus a slightly uppercut swing. Boggs, Gwynn, and I have flatter swings that complement our line-drive approach to hitting.

Let's take a closer look at each of these great hitters.

Wade Boggs

The most disciplined hitter to come into the American League in years, Wade has an idea of what he wants to do every time he comes to the plate, and the discipline, the ability to wait for a pitch, that will let him do it. Because of his discipline, you can't pitch to Wade any one way. He can lay off pitches that aren't *exactly* where he wants them. As you can see from the consistency he's shown during his first four years, it's worked for him. I don't think there is any pitcher in the American League he can't handle. Wade is only now starting to get rec-

Courtesy of Wade Boggs

Wade Boggs is a successful hitter because he is a disciplined hitter. He is never out of control at the plate. Of all the players in the game today, Wade has the best chance of anyone to accumulate five, six, or seven batting titles.

ognition, and I hope he gets a lot more, because he deserves it. He's a quiet man who just goes out and gets his one or two hits every day.

Because of his discipline, Wade has taken a rap for not hitting certain pitches in certain situations. He's been accused of always waiting for *the* perfect pitch. If I were Wade Boggs, I wouldn't change a thing. Each hitter has to find himself at the plate, and Wade has found what works for him. I also understand that much has been written about Wade's not driving in runs. I'm sensitive to this, because the same has been said about me. But hitting is something you do for the team, to help it win. Wade is never going to knock in a lot of runs batting first or second in the lineup. But during a full season, a good ballclub will score around 800 runs. During that season, Wade Boggs will score 100 runs and drive in another 50. That means he's had a hand in 150 of his team's 800 runs: nearly 20 percent. A player who does that doesn't have to apologize to anyone. Boggs does what the ballclub needs when they need it. That's how I measure a hitter.

Wade won two batting titles in his first four years. His first kept me from winning my eighth. I hit .339, good enough to win most years, but it wasn't even close. Because of the kind of hitter he is, a contact hitter who uses the whole field, Wade Boggs has the best chance of anyone playing today of going on to win five, six, or even seven batting titles.

George Brett

A thinking man's hitter. A pitcher can't throw George the same pitch two or three times in a row, because George will adjust and take advantage of a pitch thrown once too often. George sets up with his weight back, as I do, but uses a more pronounced closed front toe to help him stay in. He has a great approach into the ball, uses his hands well, and hits the ball to the opposite field as well as anyone. Because of his great hands and hitting knowledge, you rarely see George fooled by a pitch.

He's also a very, very aggressive hitter. And that makes George even tougher in clutch situations. More than any of the others we're talking about, George, like Reggie Jackson and Pete Rose, is an extrovert who likes the limelight and seems to feed off it. I first noticed that the year George was flirting with hitting .400. He enjoyed the attention more than I did in 1977. And 1985 was another example of how George carried his team when in the national spotlight—to a World Championship!

There is one other interesting thing hitters can learn from George Brett. During the prime of his career, in 1984, George "slumped" to .284 and 13 home runs. It was a year George played injured and maybe had some problems with his weight. George does sometimes play hurt, perhaps even to the detriment of his team, although his intentions are otherwise. He never let his "off year" affect him, although some foolishly questioned his desire. There are years you will be injured, and years you'll hit the ball hard but right at someone. George had that kind of year in 1984. But in watching him that year, I noticed George still had the good mechanics going for him. I knew he'd be back and expected him to have a big year in 1985. He did.

Tony Gwynn

Since he plays in the National League, I don't see as much of Tony as I do of the others. But I have seen Tony in spring training, on television and videotape, and he's impressive. Like Boggs and me, he uses his hands exceptionally well. In particular, Tony does a good job of taking the inside pitch to the left side. I'd say he's in the same category of hitting as I am. When I see Tony, it seems he has the up the middle/opposite field idea going through his mind at all times. He also works a pitcher very well. His hand action lets him spoil a lot of good pitches and extend his time at bat until he can get a good pitch to hit. That's the sign of a good hitter.

I've also noticed how Tony wiggles his bat behind his head

It's no accident that Tony Gwynn is one of the best young hitters in baseball. Look at how steady his body is, and note the extension of his arms and the lack of head movement after contact. He may be the best hitter in the National League.

when he's set in the batter's box. This is not something that coaches teach, but it underscores what this book is all about— finding out what works for you. Tony's bat wiggle helps him to stay loose, but it also serves as a timing mechanism to start his swing. For me, as we've said, it's the churning of my hands.

I live in Anaheim, only sixty miles from San Diego, and noticed that Tony got quite a bit of publicity in 1985, after hitting .351 to lead the League the year before. I read often how people, Tony included, are disappointed that he dropped off to the low .300s in 1985 (he finished the season at .315). As he plays longer, he'll realize what a great accomplishment it is to hit .300 in the major leagues. You can't hit .351 each year. If you can hit .300 year in and year out, you're a great hitter, because it gets harder every year you're in the league. Mechanically, Tony is very sound. He does, however, seem to be a little rigid in his legs. If he can work at getting a little more flexibility in those legs, he'll be more effective on lower pitches and a bigger headache to National League pitchers. Tony Gwynn has not won his last batting title. He may be the best hitter in the National League.

Don Mattingly

Don is the best young hitter I've seen in a long time. He's the type of hitter who really stays within himself. He's got good power and uses the whole field. In late 1985, Don went on a hitting tear that was unbelievable. While everyone noticed all the home runs, the thing that impressed me the most was all the singles and doubles to the opposite field. Don never went away from the basics during his hot streak. He hits the ball well to *all* fields and is not easily fooled. Despite his young age, Mattingly is already one of the toughest outs going. He is so confident at the plate that you can just feel it in the field. Like me, he knows he's good, and he wants the pitcher to know it. Don is the only other player I've seen make major adjustments to his stance during a game. The episode against Candelaria, mentioned earlier, illustrates this point. Like most of the hitters we're talking about, Don starts with his weight on his back leg. His closed front toe is similar to Brett's. And, like George, he has a slightly uppercut swing.

Don is a mature, unexcitable hitter, which you don't normally see in someone twenty-four years old. That's another reason he's such a great clutch hitter. I like the way Don handles himself as a person and as a hitter, as though he's been in the league ten years. Wait until you see the statistics he piles up when he has!

Eddie Murray

The best all-around hitter in baseball, Eddie Murray is today's Mickey Mantle, a switch-hitter with speed, power, and a .300 average. Eddie is a tough hitter who won't let himself be fooled or intimidated by a pitcher. Knock him down and he'll get up twice as determined to beat you. He's one of those rare players who are able to "find themselves" from both sides of the plate. He seems to have a little more power from the left side, but he can knock runs in from either side, as the Angels found out in 1985 when Eddie had 9 RBIs against us in one game.

Eddie has a good eye at the plate, is selective, and walks a lot. Even so, he's a very aggressive hitter, as you can see from his strikeout totals. In fact, Eddie's strikeout total dropped from 87 in 1984 to only 68 in 1985, while his home runs and RBIs rose to 31 and 124.

Boggs, Gwynn, and Mattingly are brilliant young players who have excelled in the early stages of their careers. But they are still relatively new to the big leagues. Because Eddie Murray has done it so well for so long from both sides of the plate, he has to be considered in a class by himself as a hitter.

Thirteen

———————— ◆ ————————

CAREW ON CAREW

You could say I got a rolling start in life. It was October 1, 1945, and my mother was on a train headed for a clinic when she went into labor. Luckily, there was a nurse—who later became my godmother—on the train and she provided a helping hand, or two. Hard to believe, but in appreciation of this woman's kindness, my mother seriously considered naming me Margaret Ann after her. Thankfully, there was a doctor aboard and he finished up the delivery. His name was Rodney Cline. I became Rodney Cline Carew. Can you imagine all the fights I would have had defending a name like Margaret Ann?

I spent my early years in Gatun, a little town of 2,000 near the Panama Canal. When you grow up in a Latin American country, especially in a small town, there really isn't much to do. We didn't have a swimming pool, so many of us ended up swimming in the Canal, a dubious proposition because of the presence of alligators and ships slipping through the locks. Quite a few of my friends had accidents in the Canal, so to keep out of harm's way we turned to sports—everything from volleyball to soccer.

Baseball, however, was my first love. I began playing at five, using an old broomstick for a bat. We were so poor that major-league bats and balls were out of the question. So we improvised, painting broomsticks different colors, imitating our fa-

169

vorite American players (mine were Willie Mays and Jackie Robinson), playing out our fantasies in the streets, with tennis balls, and paper bags for gloves. And if for some reason nobody wanted to play, I'd throw a ball against the steps of our apartment for hours, never stopping until dark.

Later on, when I was eight, we moved away from Gatun to Gamboa, a couple of miles south of the Canal. Again, the life-style wasn't much, a five-room wooden apartment filled with my father, mother, brother, and two sisters. Like everyone else, I'm a product of my upbringing. I was a very sick child growing up—I had rheumatic fever—and my father never really thought I was tough enough. I was in and out of the hospital a lot, something that irritated him because he believed little boys should be tough (like my brother), so I was physically abused at times. I mean, there wasn't a time in my life I wasn't kicked, or punched, or whipped, often for no reason whatsoever. Certainly I was good in school; I never caused my parents problems; I never fought. But for some reason my father chose to pick on me, and, to be honest, it affected my personality. I think it's one reason I'm so reticent with the press today, so cautious about opening up to others. When you're young and under attack, you withdraw from family and friends. So shyness stays with you in later years.

As time went on, my mother kept in close contact with my godmother, who, it turns out, lived in New York. One day, when I was fourteen or so, my godmother asked if I wanted to come to the United States and finish my education. I wanted to leave Panama at the time because I knew that after graduation from school most kids did very little. I didn't want to just exist, I wanted to be *somebody*, and I knew that if given half a chance, with my baseball abilities, I could make something of myself after finishing high school in New York.

I'll never forget looking out the airplane window on my first trip into New York Harbor. It was dark, the city aglow, a blaze of light; I had the feeling a whole new world was opening up to me. Sure, I was a little scared; I knew of the problems any person faces in New York—particularly someone just four-teen. But my mother was already there, so I adjusted quickly, learning the ropes, how to ride the subways, what buses to take, the dangers of being in the wrong place at the right time.

The one thing I can still remember both my mother and god-mother drilling into my head was the danger of succumbing to peer pressure. I think that's one reason so many kids have problems today. They want to be liked, to fit in, so they follow the leader. But there are problems with following others. A lot of times you can end up staring at a dead end. Soon after immi-grating to New York I enrolled at George Washington High School in the Bronx. I had a hard time learning English, spend-ing so much time on the new language that I wasn't able to try out for the high-school baseball team—and anyway, the coach had already told me to forget it, that I wasn't good enough to make his club. So I played sandlot ball instead, which was fine. It gave me the confidence I needed. I can still remember lying in my bed, listening to Armed Forces Radio at night, dreaming about the day I would play in Yankee Stadium or a World Se-ries (I'm still dreaming about that last one; maybe next year, right?). The dream drove me, day after day, swing after swing. I knew if given half a chance I would make it no matter what a high-school coach had said. As time went on, scouts from a half-dozen different teams—the Chicago White Sox, Detroit Ti-gers, Chicago Cubs, New York Yankees, Pittsburgh Pirates, and, of course, the Minnesota Twins—started showing up at my games. There was never any doubt in those days about what I wanted to do after high school: I wanted to sign. The sooner the better.

I'll never forget that signing day. It was graduation day in a lot of ways—from high school and from amateur baseball. I remember sitting at graduation ceremonies, staring at my watch every few seconds, thinking, "Let's get this thing over with right now." Sure enough, right after graduation, a Minnesota Twins scout took my uncle and me out to dinner. The scout asked how much it would take to get me to sign. I didn't care and said, "Let's just get this thing over with, because I'm ready to sign, get on an airplane, and play ball somewhere." But my uncle, thank goodness, had a more level head. He took me aside and said, "Let's find out the specifics of the contract." Once we did, I still couldn't write my name fast enough. I wanted to play ball.

Now, looking back on more than two decades of my professional career, certain memories do shine through. Certainly making the All-Star team my first year was a highlight. Just standing on the same field with Ernie Banks, Mays, Mantle— men I had idolized—made my knees shake.

My biggest thrill, however, has to be my first major-league hit! It came off Dave McNally of the Orioles on my second big league at-bat. I know it's hard to believe Number 3,000 doesn't top the list, but honestly, when you get that first hit it means you belong. You can relax. You've proved you can play, even if it's only for the moment. I've stayed around for quite some time, fortunately, but believe me, it's done nothing to diminish the excitement of that first base hit. My 3,000th hit? Well, just being mentioned in the same breath with Rose, Cobb, Rogers Hornsby, and Roberto Clemente is almost as gratifying. After all, there are only sixteen athletes in our little club, and I consider it an honor to be included in the membership.

Another honor related to that 3,000th hit came in November 1985, when I was asked by the government in Panama to return for a celebration. As part of the event I was given that nation's Medal of Honor by the Panamanian president, and my number—29—was permanently retired. That means no player, at any level and in any sport, can wear that number in Panama. It was a heartwarming experience for someone who has purposely kept his Panamanian citizenship in hopes of giving the youth of that country a role model. The sights and sounds of that trip will never be forgotten.

One thing I'm often asked during interviews is what I've learned from my time in the game, what experience I would like to share with others. One thing I've certainly discovered is the importance of humility. Unlike most doctors, lawyers, and teachers, athletes perform in the full view of the press and public. Often our achievements—no more distinguished, really, than what goes on in some operating rooms or classrooms—are elevated to unrealistic levels. That's why I believe in humility. Sure, when I go out on the field, I'm a so-called star, but when I come off, I try to be just like everyone else leaving his or her job. I want to go home to my family and kids.

Humility is one of the main reasons I sympathize with fans who boo or cheer. To me, by virtue of their admission ticket, they have an inalienable right to let off steam, to derive some satisfaction from sport. And if writing my name on a piece of paper is going to make some youngster look up to me or bring a smile to someone's face, then I'm going to do it. And keep on doing it until folks stop asking.

Finally, in the preceding chapter I touched upon some of the finest hitters in the game today. But I would be remiss if I didn't include players like Tony Oliva and Frank Robinson on my all-time hitter list. Oliva could do so much with the bat; he played in pain; he showed me the meaning of the word "pro." Robbie, too. After seeing Frank come over from the National League, watching how he went about his job, full tilt, giving himself up when the situation called for it, you couldn't help but be impressed. Here was a textbook player, a future Hall of Famer, doing whatever it took to win. I should also add Reggie Jackson to this list. Reggie's drive, his intensity, and the impact he has on a team and a game are second to none.

And what about the toughest pitchers I've faced? Well, you know about Rudy May. Over the years, Ron Guidry of the Yankees has also been very tough on me. He's left-handed, throws hard, can spot a wicked slider, and is very smart. But Ron had been tough on everybody. Through 1985 his won-loss record was 154-68 in 11 seasons, including 22 wins in 1985 at the age of 35. There are several other pitchers I've gained great respect for over the years—Catfish Hunter, Jim Palmer, and Denny McClain among them. They all shared the same strengths:

Hall of Famer Roy Campanella said, "You have to have a lot of little boy in you to play this game." I couldn't agree more. Work hard, but have fun doing it.

They didn't beat themselves, always came right after you, didn't walk many guys, and kept the ball in play, relying on the excellent athletes playing behind them.

In closing, I know some of you might be wondering what I'm like off the field. Well, I'm a loving husband, a devoted dad, and a photography buff in my spare time. I'm also a firm believer in putting something back into the game that's willed me so much. I spend a lot of the off-season doing charity and community work, putting on clinics, or just helping some organization that can benefit from my name. But basically I just try to be Rod Carew, the person, whether it's sitting around the house, enjoying the company of my wife and daughters, watching TV or a movie, or going for a boat ride, anything to unwind from the pressures of playing baseball.

At this point, I sincerely hope you understand me a little more, and certainly my philosophies about hitting. Writing this book has been an enjoyable—and educational—experience. I hope some of my ideas wear off, and you'll begin to improve both your physical and mental approach to the game. I've always wanted to pass along something that, in part, God gave me the ability and desire to do. I hope in some real way this book helps transfer some of that ability and desire to your game. Good luck, work hard, and happy hitting!

CAREW'S CAREER

Highlights

- Became 16th man in major-league history to reach 3,000 career hits, on August 4, 1985
- 7-time American League batting champion
- 1977 American League Most Valuable Player
- 18-time American League All-Star
- Batted over .300 15 years in a row
- All-time major-league All-Star vote getter, with over 32,000,000 votes
- Batted .388 in 1977 with 239 hits
- Batted .344 for the decade 1970–79
- Has surpassed 200 hits in a season 4 times
- Currently 13th on the all-time major-league hit list
- Stole home 17 times in his career, including 7 in 1969
- Has 896 career multiple-hit games (2 hits or more), including 51 4-hit games
- Has 5 career grand-slam home runs
- Stole 49 bases in 1976
- Drove in 100 runs in 1977
- Played in 4 American League Championship Series
- .328 career batting average in 19 seasons
- Drove in 1,000th run during 1985

- Hit for cycle (single, double, triple, and home runs in one game) June 20, 1970
- Ranks 28th in career games played
- Ranks 6th in career one-base hits

Lifetime Batting Record

YR	CLUB	AVG	G	AB	R	H	2B	3B	HR	RBI	BB	SO	SB
1967	MN	.292	137	514	66	150	22	7	8	51	37	91	5
1968	MN	.273	127	461	46	126	27	2	1	42	26	71	12
1969	MN	.332	123	458	79	152	30	4	8	56	37	72	19
1970	MN	.366	51	191	27	70	12	3	4	28	11	28	4
1971	MN	.307	147	577	88	177	16	10	2	48	45	81	6
1972	MN	.318	142	535	61	170	21	6	0	51	43	60	12
1973	MN	.350	149	580	98	203	30	11	6	62	62	55	41
1974	MN	.364	153	599	86	218	30	5	3	55	74	49	38
1975	MN	.359	143	535	89	192	24	4	14	80	64	40	35
1976	MN	.331	156	605	97	200	29	12	9	90	67	52	49
1977	MN	.388	155	616	128	239	38	16	14	100	69	55	23
1978	MN	.333	152	564	85	188	26	10	5	70	78	62	27
1979	CA	.318	110	409	78	130	15	3	3	44	73	46	18
1980	CA	.331	144	540	74	179	34	7	3	59	59	38	23
1981	CA	.305	93	364	57	111	17	1	2	21	45	45	6
1982	CA	.319	138	523	88	167	25	5	3	44	67	49	10
1983	CA	.339	129	472	66	160	24	2	2	44	57	48	6
1984	CA	.295	93	329	42	97	8	1	3	31	40	39	4
1985	CA	.280	127	443	69	124	17	3	2	39	64	47	5
MAJOR LEAGUE TOTALS:		.328	2469	9315	1424	3053	445	112	92	1015	1018	1028	353